# VICTORIAN DESIGN
# SOURCE
# BOOK

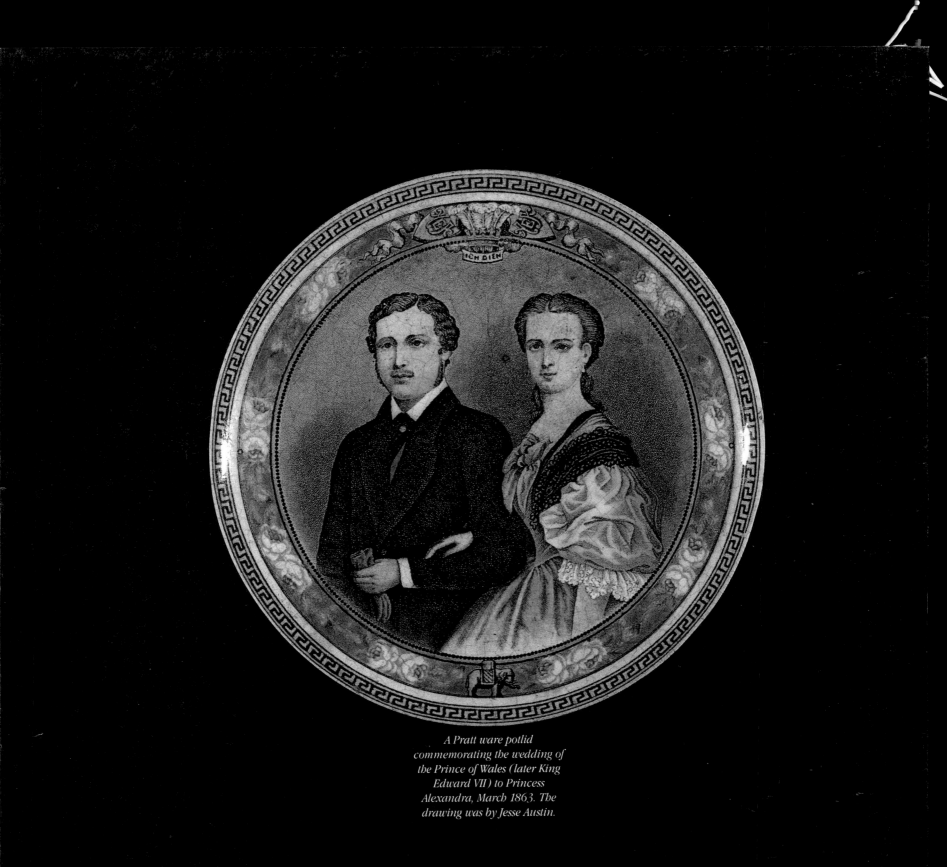

*A Pratt ware potlid commemorating the wedding of the Prince of Wales (later King Edward VII) to Princess Alexandra, March 1863. The drawing was by Jesse Austin.*

# VICTORIAN DESIGN
# SOURCE
# BOOK

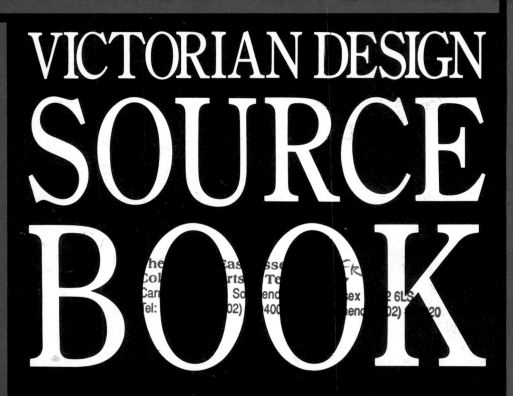

## NOËL RILEY

A QUARTO BOOK

Published by Phaidon Press Limited
Musterlin House
Jordan Hill Road
Oxford OX2 8DP

First published 1989
Copyright © 1989 Quarto Publishing plc

A CIP catalogue record for this book is available
from the British Library

ISBN 0 7148 2602 2

This book was designed and produced by
Quarto Publishing plc
The Old Brewery, 6 Blundell Street
London N7 9BH

**Project Editor** Hazel Harrison
**Editor** James Clark
**Design** Hazel Edington
**Picture Research** Chris Saunders

**Art Director** Moira Clinch
**Editorial Director** Carolyn King

Typeset by Text Filmsetters Ltd., London
and QV Typesetters, London
Manufactured in Hong Kong by
Regent Publishing Services Ltd
**Printed in Hong Kong by South Sea Int'l Press Ltd.**

# CONTENTS

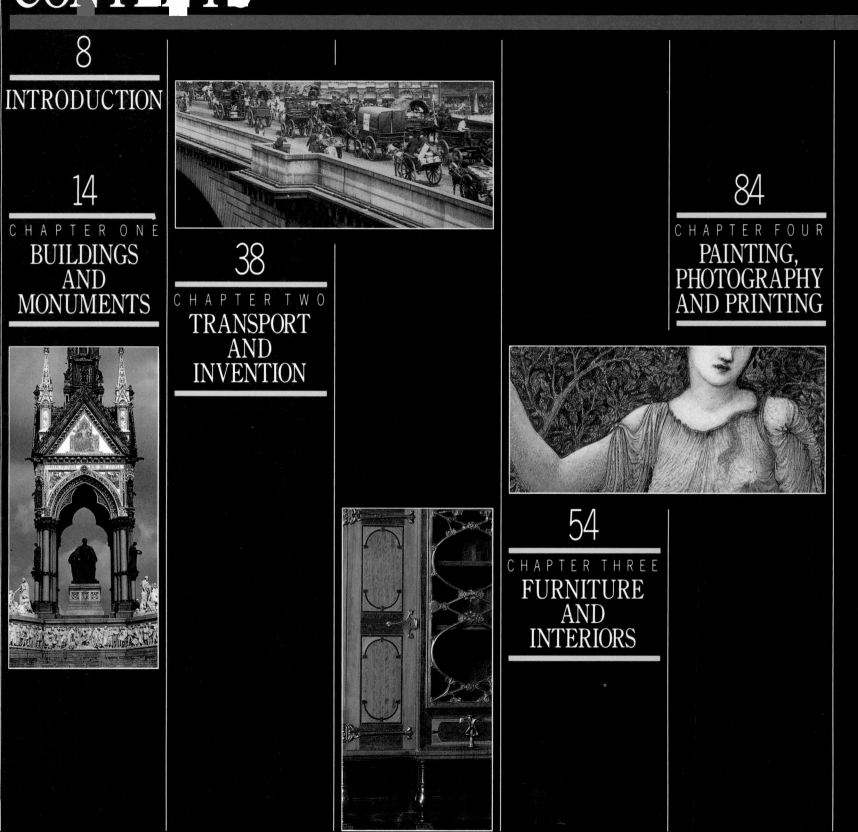

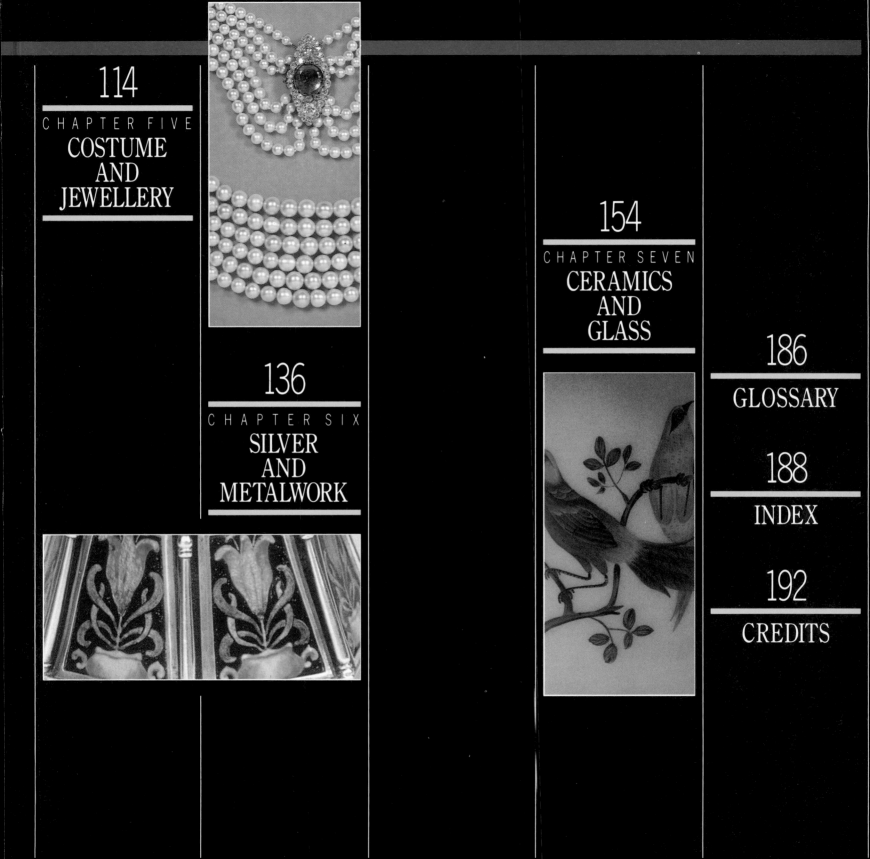

# INTRODUCTION

**(1)** *A design for a choir screen for Salisbury Cathedral in the "Ecclesiological" style by George Gilbert Scott. A symptom of the subsequent devaluation of all* *things Victorian is the fact that in 1959 this astonishing piece of Gothic revival craftmanship was removed and sold to a metal dealer. It has only been* *during the last twenty years or so that 19th-century art has become widely appreciated.*

**V**ictorian design, to most people, means carved walnut furniture, towering centrepieces of glass and silver, heftily draped fabrics of purple, maroon or moss green and dark, stuffy rooms. It means the Houses of Parliament and the Albert Memorial, deep-buttoned Chesterfields, piles of wax fruit under glass domes, antimacassars, hall stands and aspidistras. It is easy to forget that Victorian design is also the Crystal Palace, Thonet chairs, Christopher Dresser metalwork, Godwin furniture and Morris textiles.

The Victorian period was one of unprecedented contrasts: between immense wealth and squalid poverty; between rampant historicism and an almost obsessional quest for a "19th-century style"; between powered vehicles and horse-drawn transport; between glorification of the machine and wholehearted condemnation of the enslaving drudgery it brought; between the spiritual quest and the technological thrust; between complacency and self-criticism, pomposity and humility, and between the earnestness of A.W.N. Pugin and the humour of William Burges.

Design was affected by the coming of the railways as much as by developments in steam-powered machinery, while events abroad as well as economic fluctuations at home played a considerable part. The continental turmoils of 1848 and 1870 caused many artists and technicians to seek refuge in Britain. They made their mark in art schools and ceramic factories or, like James Tissot and Lawrence Alam-Tadema, became celebrated "British" painters.

Momentous advances — the railways, photography, motor cars, steel and glass technology, wireless telegraphy and electricity — must be seen against the Victorians' relentless fascination with the past. It was as if they were frightened by their own technical and industrial prowess and felt a need to reassure themselves by going backwards in history for their styles. It was not until late in the 19th century that the Victorians began to unshackle themselves from slavish historicism and move towards truly progressive design. While the majority of styles were based on historical re-interpretations of one form or another, the huge surge of technical development affected both the kinds of objects that were made and the way in which they were fashioned.

### Collecting and faking

The particular course of Victorian historicism was affected to a considerable extent by a relatively new activity — antique collecting. Of course collectors had existed since Renaissance times, but those who were not of the princely classes were mainly preoccupied with "curiosities" or with the acquisition of oriental ceramics and other objects from the Far East. The dispersals of European furniture and *objets d'art* following the French Revolution stimu-

2

but also, at local levels, to ruthless pillaging of sites. Cottage industries sprang up to make cheap but often attractive copies, while more "expert" enterprises produced carefully "antiqued" forgeries, designed to deceive — and to fetch high prices.

### The question of taste

Industrial and technological growth had begun long before Queen Victoria's reign, but by the 1840s it had reached satanic proportions and was accompanied by a corresponding entrenchment of capitalism. Mercantile success was proclaimed in the quantity of objects available and in their showiness. For the new prosperous classes — both producing and consuming — ornament, and plenty of it, was more important than suitability of design. This worried the artistic élite, who perceived their mission to be the improvement of general standards of design and the imposition of "good taste" on both the public and industry. As one contemporary lamented in 1844: "We have only to compare the productions of France and Germany with our own and we shall find that their staples are all connected with *taste* and that our staples are those of quantity."

It was assumed by the "improvers" that the raising of artistic levels would be followed by moral improvement as a matter of course. As well as this ethical view of the benefits of better artistic standards, there was another: simply that good design brought higher financial dividends. The fact that new machines were constantly being developed

*(2) This terracotta figure purporting to be from Tanagra in Greece and made c. 500 BC was in fact made in the 1870s, when excavations were being carried out in Boeotia. This attractive fake is now a collectors' piece in its own right.*

*(3) A piano panel painted with a classical scene by Sir Lawrence Alma-Tadema, one of the most successful of 19th-century immigrant artists. He was Dutch by birth, but settled in England in 1870.*

lated a new wave of collecting which was well established by the 1830s, and had particular relevance for both the Gothic and Rococo revivals.

The acquisition by rich English and American collectors of luxurious 18th-century French furniture ensured the prestige — and the continued reproduction — of French furniture styles. Similarly, collectors of medieval art, and Pugin was a significant example, encouraged the re-use of fragments of carving or panelling in Victorian furniture, or the accurate copying of medieval details in metal or stone. Collectors of paintings began to look further back, to the Italian and Northern European primitive schools, a fashion of great interest in relation to Pre-Raphaelitism.

Eighteenth-century and earlier European ceramics were widely collected, and many of the 19th-century historical revivals were based on pieces which had been hunted out by connoisseurs. While many were genuine copies or revivals, not intended to deceive, a lively market in ceramic forgery began to grow up towards the end of the century. The high-quality porcelain reproductions of Samson of Paris and Carle Thieme of Potschappel, for example, are now collectors' pieces in their own right. The thirst for archaeological fragments and artefacts was insatiable, and led not only to the enriching of museums

**1**

*(1) A Royal Worcester "Aesthetic" teapot, 1881, with an Oscar Wilde figure on one side and an aesthetically costumed lady on the other. This rare example of humour in ceramics pokes fun at the aesthetes in much the same way as the Gilbert and Sullivan operetta* Patience.

The debate about the relationship between art and manufactures, that is, between commercial needs and the demands of what the Victorians perceived to be good taste, ran and ran. It was at its height in the 1830s and '40s, and in 1836 a Government committee examined the subject from the point of view of manufacturers, artists, connoisseurs and art dealers. One of its direct results was the setting up of the Government School of Design at Somerset House in 1837. Its object was to "educate in art", but emphatically not to produce practitioners of the fine arts.

In 1840 Government grants were provided for establishing more schools of design, in Manchester, Birmingham, Glasgow, Paisley and Leeds, while at the same time the setting up of museums and collections accessible to all, including the working classes, was called for.

Another thrust in the direction of raising public taste had been made in 1836 with the founding of the Art Union

to enable the production of more embellishment at less expense in no way diminished the problem, and where machinery was lacking there was no shortage of technical skill or cheap labour — so the improvers had an uphill struggle.

It must be remembered, however, that critics of taste in the 19th century wielded power to a degree inconceivable today. In an age without television or radio the influence of public lectures and the written word on a newly prosperous and socially aspiring section of the population was considerable. Thus John Ruskin, with his mastery of prose, could in a large measure dictate the taste of his period, whether in architecture or painting.

Ruskin was not the only arbiter, although his was undoubtedly the most powerful voice in the middle decades of the century. Pugin, Prince Albert, Henry Cole, Charles Locke Eastlake and Owen Jones were influential too, through public works and publications.

Ironically, the Great Exhibition of 1851, conceived as *the* great fillip to the improvement of design, proved to be the century's main manifestation of ostentatious vulgarity and, far from spawning a range of well-designed things for "general use", it gave rise to the "exhibition object" — of absurd splendour and virtuoso craftsmanship.

**2**

*(2) Roland Hill's introduction of the penny postage in 1840 revolutionized the postal system. For the first time, letters were pre-paid, and went for the same rate to any destination in Britain. The world's first postage stamp, the Penny Black, was closely followed by the Twopence Blue for letters weighing more than half an ounce. The design of the Queen's head which appeared on both (and on other stamps for the rest of her reign) was taken from a medal by William Wyon, former chief engraver to the Royal Mint.*

of London, a society whose members participated in a lottery with works of art such as paintings, prints, bronzes and parian porcelain sculptures as prizes. Public response, at least among the well-to-do, was encouraging, and other art unions followed.

In 1849 Henry Cole made a similarly evangelistic gesture by commissioning artists to design attractive and unpretentious glass, ceramics and silver for everyday use, and decorative parian figures; with them he launched Felix Summerly's Art Manufactures as a commercial venture. Cole himself spread his net widely: he wrote children's books, designed glass, and was a vigorous campaigner for reforms ranging from the postal service to public health; later he was to be the chief reformer of the national design schools and the founder of what is now the Victoria and Albert Museum.

### Exhibitions

Exhibitions were added to all the other efforts to inject the elusive magic ingredient of good taste into British manufactures. The idea was not new. The French had organized the first large-scale exhibition of industry and industrial art in 1798 and had followed it with many more. Industrial centres such as Manchester, Birmingham and Dublin held their own during the 1820s, '30s and '40s.

In 1843 Prince Albert, already deeply involved in the movement to improve industrial design, became president of the Royal Society of Arts, one of whose successes had been the running of design competitions. As a development of this, Prince Albert and his staunch ally, Henry Cole, initiated a series of exhibitions of "British Art Manufactures" in 1847. By 1849 the concept had emerged of a bigger-than-ever exhibition, international in scope and funded by voluntary subscription rather than by taxation. The Great Exhibition of the Works of Industry of all Nations was born. It was to be both the biggest exhibition ever held and the first to be international: industrial arts, raw materials and machinery were amassed from all over the world.

The project generated typically Victorian extremes. On the one hand there was unstinting enthusiasm and support, while on the other there was venomous opposition from those who prophesied that the inevitable influx of foreigners would bring damage and destruction to property, outbreaks of immorality and cholera and, worst of all, revolution. The actual event proved to be enormously successful both commercially and as a stimulant to manufacture, and it concentrated the national mind on design. As usual, the camps were deeply divided between those who, like the Queen, thought the Exhibition had "quite the effect of fairyland" and those who saw it as the greatest-ever display of design anarchy, "a fruitless struggle after novelty, irrespective of fitness", as Owen Jones put it.

The Great Exhibition was followed in 1857 by the

*3*

*(3) Poverty and destitution were as common in Victorian England as prosperity, and many were forced to emigrate, often to a very uncertain future. Ford Madox Brown's haunting Pre-Raphaelite image of his friend the sculptor Thomas Woolner with his wife Emma on their way to Australia,* The Last of England, *was painted in 1860. As he wrote: "I have ... singled out a couple from the middle classes, high enough, through education and refinement, to appreciate all they are now giving up, and yet depressed enough in means to have to put up with the discomforts and humiliations incident to a vessel 'all one class'."*

**(1)** An ebonized chair with a
cane seat designed by E.W.
Godwin and probably made by
William Watt, whose catalogue,
Art Furniture, was published in
1877. Godwin's Japanese-
inspired designs for furniture
were highly influential and led
to the widespread use of
ebonized finishes.

**(2)** A scarlet tortoiseshell and
ormolu-mounted cabinet
signed by the Parisian
manufacturer of decorative
metalwork Charles Stanislas
Matifat, 1849. It is a typically
ornate but finely executed
example of "exhibition"
furniture.

Manchester Art Treasures Exhibition, in which Prince Albert
was again closely involved. For this, works of art were
assembled from private collections all over England,
including those of Queen Victoria and Prince Albert. Its
express purpose was to "instruct the uneducated in art
history" and by so doing elevate public taste and thereby
design in manufacture. How far it succeeded is impossible
to measure, but it was visited by over a million people and
it set a didactic precedent for almost all public art exhibitions since.

Industrial exhibitions, both national and international,
continued for the rest of the century — again in London in
1862, and in Dublin, Paris, Brussels, Munich, Vienna, Philadelphia and Chicago, to name a few. Their influence on
the course of design was effected largely through the pres-

2

tige and commercial success they brought to individual
manufacturers whose products won medals. They were
often more significant in showing off technology and
craftmanship than in reforming design.

### New movements
The catalytic effect of the Great Exhibition and its suc-
cessor gave a clear focus to the teachings of Ruskin and
the Gothic revivalists who advocated a return to craft-
based vernacular traditions with their emphasis on functional design and honesty of craftsmanship. Their call was
taken up and transformed by William Morris, whose idealized medievalism had social as well as design implic-
ations. His view of the machine as the enslaver of working
people has been derided as unrealistic, and the fact that
he was obliged to spend much of his working life "minis-
tering to the swinish luxury of the rich" has been scorned
as inconsistent, yet his socialistic teachings still have a pro-
phetic relevance a century later.

1

In its affirmation of the central importance of hand-craftsmanship, Morris's philosophy succeeded in blurring the division between the fine and the applied arts. His disciples included Crane, Ashbee, Mackmurdo, Day, Benson, Shaw, Lethaby and Voysey, and they carried his design principles into the 20th century. Many of them exhibited their works through the Arts and Crafts Exhibition Society, founded in 1888, or worked within groups such as the Century Guild, the Art Workers Guild and the Guild of Handicraft.

The London International Exhibition of 1862 was notable in two respects: it included contributions from Morris's newly established firm, Morris, Marshall, Faulkner & Co., and it displayed, for the first time to most Europeans, the art and artefacts of Japan. They made an immediate impact, and resulted in the design phenomenon known as the Aesthetic Movement.

Designers like Christopher Dresser, E.W. Godwin and Eden Nesfield turned with relish from the interminable historicism of the preceding decades to forms and motifs that seemed wholly fresh and original. By the 1870s "Japanism" was to be seen in the design of all kinds of commercially produced objects as well as those of hand-craftsmen.

But during the 1890s, aestheticism eventually became submerged under Art Nouveau. This was a direct outcome of the Arts and Crafts Movement, and its sinuous organic quality was already discernible in the designs of Mackmurdo during the 1880s. In 1895 the art dealer and patron Samuel Bing, an authority on Japanese art, opened a gallery in Paris specializing in the new style: he called it La Maison de l'Art Nouveau. Bing was not just significant in providing the name: by his patronage of designers like van der Velde, Lalique, Gallé, Tiffany and Colonna as well as Crane, Mackintosh, Morris, Benson, Voysey and Brangwyn, he ensured its rapid adoption as an international decorative style.

*(3) Design for a textile (1898) by Lewis F. Day, whose other designs included stained glass, wallpaper, tiles, furniture, silver and jewellery. Day was a friend of William Morris, a founder of the Art Worker's Guild and a prolific journalist.*

3

*Bronze statue of Richard I (Coeur de Lion) by Baron Carlo Marochetti erected in 1860 in New Palace Yard, Westminster.*

# CHAPTER ONE
# BUILDINGS AND MONUMENTS

*(1)* *A workhouse building in Endell Street, London, designed by Lee & Smith in 1879. A modified Gothic style was obviously regarded as suitable for an institution whose role was often of a moralizing flavour.*

The sheer volume of building during the Victorian period is awesome. As a result of the Industrial Revolution huge cities emerged from small communities; populations in Europe and North America exploded and the necessity for new building — for housing, offices, churches, factories, public and educational institutions and engineering schemes — was matched by the money to pay for it.

The Victorian period was one of unprecedented growth in public building, much of it taking the form of unabashed monuments of civic pride, individual grandeur or showy altruism. Government and municipal buildings, hospitals, libraries, museums and galleries, universities, railway stations, theatres, banks and hotels began to appear where formerly only a sprinkling of town halls, prisons, workhouses and schools had represented community building. Large-scale memorials to national heroes such as the Duke of Wellington, Sir Walter Scott and Albert, the Prince Consort were designed in the form of great Gothic or Classical shrines.

The building trade was a vast one (in England it employed about six per cent of the labour force), but while the social status of the architect was high, that of the builder was little regarded. One exception was Thomas Cubitt, the great housing speculator who made his mark most visibly on Belgravia and Pimlico in London.

But the majority of building firms were relatively small and their varying methods and practices were only gradually brought under a measure of control by municipal building regulations introduced to ensure standards of health, workmanship and suitability of materials. Relatively uncontrolled were the dense areas of poor housing in the industrial and mining areas of the Midlands and north of Britain, where scant attention was paid to the inhabitants' welfare. Efforts to ameliorate the living conditions of the workers were made by certain individuals, and the Society for Improving the Conditions of the Labouring Classes (founded in 1844) was one of several such organizations. A few manufacturers also saw the wisdom of providing good housing for their employees. Woollens millionaire Titus Salt built a model town around his mills, called Saltaire, near Leeds (1851-76); the cocoa dynasty of the Cadburys created Bournville (begun 1879), and W.H. Lever (later Lord Leverhulme), created Port Sunlight on Merseyside (begun 1888).

### Mechanization

The development of transport, and the mechanization of the brick industry during the 1850s and 1860s were added spurs to the building trade. With the ability to carry bricks, slates, stone and other goods relatively cheaply by rail or canal, builders and architects no longer had to confine themselves to local materials.

1

The new steam-powered cranes and saws made both quarrying and processing natural materials easier, while building timber from North America and the Baltic became widely and cheaply available throughout Europe. The glass and tile industries also made great strides, reflected in buildings both inside and out. The growth of the iron industry — the pride of the Industrial Revolution — made possible the rapid emergence of an entirely new architecture during the mid-19th century. In fact nearly all the truly modern buildings were the work of engineers rather than architects.

### Revival styles

However, most designers of buildings were looking to historical precedents for inspiration rather than to new techniques and materials. In France, Henri Labrouste's most adventurous use of iron (Bibliothèque Nationale, 1843-50) was an exception. It was in Chicago in the 1880s that architecture was to make its greatest leap towards the

20th century with the first steel-framed skyscrapers.

Until the first years of Victoria's reign, which began in 1837, 19th-century European architecture remained faithful to the neo-classical style, whose demure, unadorned formality was seen to represent reason, order and harmony — the "noble simplicity and calm grandeur" of Greek art. In England its leading lights included George Basevi, Decimus Burton, Robert Smirke, Charles Robert Cockerell and Charles Barry. In Germany Leo von Klenze and Carl-Friedrich Schinkel left their neo-classical stamp on Munich and Berlin respectively, while the precepts of Jean-Nicolas-Louis Durand's "classical" functionalism were respected by architects all over the Continent.

Given that every generation reacts against its immediate predecessor, it was hardly surprising that Regency classicism should provoke a strong revolt in some quarters. Many considered Classical order, symmetry and authority to be unromantic, overcontrolled and, above all, *pagan,* in contrast to the devout, medieval taste of the romantics in literature and painting. The taste for mediev-

3

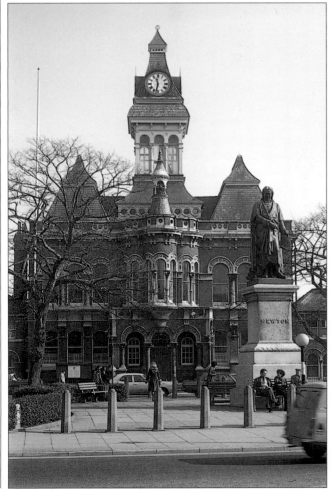

2

al mystery, sumptuousness and fantasy, which the new "Goths" encouraged, was not new. Theories on the picturesque had abounded in the 18th century, and had greatly affected garden design.

Enthusiasts for the "Gothick" style (as it was then called) had toyed with medieval motifs on what were fundamentally Georgian buildings. What was new in the 1830s was the moral earnestness and historical accuracy with which the early Victorians embraced the Gothic. From being just a style of picturesque fantasy, it was now promoted to the style of the righteous.

The chief protagonist of the Gothic Revival in England was A.W.N. Pugin, whose personal religious fervour set it on its moralizing course. To Pugin, a Roman Catholic convert, and his followers in the "ecclesiological" movement both in Britain and North America, Christianity had flourished in its most spiritually pure form during the Middle Ages, and therefore its architecture was the ideal to be followed.

The mystique of medieval church building and liturgy in the Age of Chivalry added welcome romantic associations to the Gothic style. Rich romantics housed themselves in mock-medieval castles like Anthony Salvin's Peckforton in Cheshire, while the Scottish Baronial style, seen at its most spectacular at Dunrobin in Sutherland and Balmoral in Aberdeenshire, was Gothic Revival crossed with Scottish antiquarianism.

John Ruskin, the most influential critic of the 19th century, promoted the medieval ideal in his *Seven Lamps of Architecture* (1849), adding fuel to Pugin's fire. Ruskin contended that "ornamentation is the principal part of architecture". Suitability to purpose was for him less important than the decoration of a building. In *The*

*(2) Red terracotta is contrasted with white stone and grey slate in William Watkins's Romanesque-inspired Town Hall, Grantham, with its imposing clock tower (1867-69). (3) The river front of St Thomas's Hospital, London, by Henry Currey (1868-78). St Thomas's (now substantially rebuilt) was an example of the "pavilion" type of hospital building, in which the wards were arranged in separate blocks allowing maximum light and air, as well as a degree of separation from different kinds of illness. The smaller block (second from left) is the hospital chapel.*

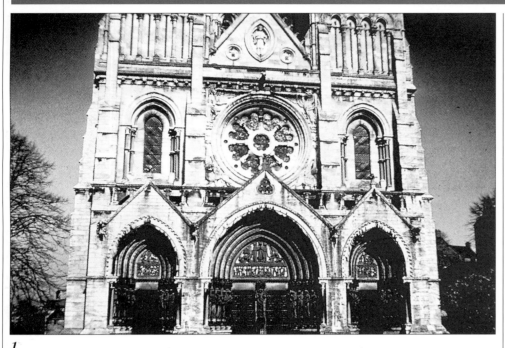

**1**

*(1) Part of the massive Gothic front of St Finn Bar's (Anglican) Cathedral, Cork, by William Burges (1863-79). He modelled it on the early Gothic cathedrals of northern France such as Chartres and Laon. (2) Victor Horta's house in Brussels, built in 1898. Although Art Nouveau is primarily a style of decoration rather than of form, the so-called Art Nouveau architects – Horta in Brussels, Guimard in Paris, Endell in Munich, Wagner and Hofmann in Vienna and, most original of all, Gaudi in Barcelona – used it to give a much-needed impetus to the departure from traditional and historicist styles. Their call was taken up particularly in Austria and Germany where the Modern Movement of the 20th century was most formatively reared.*

*Stones of Venice* (1851) he advocated the Venetian form of Gothic with its emphasis on colour and varied texture in building materials, and this was duly adopted both in Britain and North America during the 1850s and 1860s.

### A kaleidoscope of styles

The Victorians' admiration for the "Olden Time", exemplified in such publications as Joseph Nash's *Mansions of England in the Olden Time* (1838-49), gave rise to a hotch-potch of Elizabethan and Jacobean ornament superimposed on mock "Renaissance" or "Tudor" and, later, "Queen Anne" buildings. Its historical associations, however superficial and even sham, apparently gave reassurance to a generation dazzled and confused by its own unprecedented progress to status and prosperity.

Classicism persisted, in one form or another, all through the 19th century, particularly for public buildings, but it was almost invariably revivalist, like the neo-Palladian, or the neo-Italian Renaissance. The latter is exemplified by Charles Barry's Reform Club in London, and by Queen Victoria's seaside residence at Osborne on the Isle of Wight.

The English moved from the mid-Victorian Italian palazzo and "Jacobethan" styles to "Queen Anne" and neo-Rococo later in the century, while the French adopted a neo-French Renaissance style which developed into an extravagant neo-Baroque in such buildings as Charles Garnier's Opera in Paris. In Germany the term *Rundbogenstil* covered all the round-arched styles — early Christian, Romanesque and Byzantine — that were favoured there.

### The domestic revival

It was probably in domestic building during the 1830s and 1840s that the most adventurous forays into history and romance were made. J.C. Loudon published his *Encyclopaedia of Cottage, Farm and Villa Architecture and Furniture* in 1833, and this was widely influential as a design manual for builders and furniture makers.

Loudon, a man of advanced views on social and educational issues as well as an architectural pioneer and gardening expert, was the inventor of ridge and furrow construction for glasshouses, the method later adopted by Paxton for the Crystal Palace. Loudon's own house in Porchester Terrace, London, was the model for the semi-detached villa, to be followed thousands of times over. Loudon saw equal merit in the Classical and the Gothic, which he used freely, alongside "Old English" cottages, Italian villas and Swiss chalets.

### American architects

By the 1860s American architecture was beginning to pull itself from under the dominating shadow of England. Many American architects now went to France, and

**2**

specifically to the Ecole des Beaux-Arts in Paris, for their training, returning to pepper the post-Civil War U.S.A. with château-like buildings sporting mansard roofs, dormer windows, balconies and pointed turrets in what became known as the Beaux-Arts style. At the same time the tastes of a number of German and Austrian-born immigrant architects was stamped most noticeably on the new architecture of the Mid-western cities.

American architects such as Richard Morris Hunt, Henry Hobson Richardson, John Wellborn Root, Frank Furness and Louis Sullivan were enjoying world-wide respect by the late 19th century, but it was Sullivan's pupil, Frank Lloyd Wright, who commanded the greatest admiration at the start of his career. Whether in his designs for huge office blocks or small country houses — and his work ranged widely — his originality of approach has rarely been equalled.

### Vernacular architecture

One outcome of the "picturesque" and "old English" style was the revival of vernacular architecture — a move away from textbook styles back to a craft-based, regionally oriented way of building. Philip Webb, architect to William Morris and the Arts and Crafts Movement, was one of the first exponents of a craft-based or vernacular style, but most of the late 19th-century Arts and Crafts sympathizers, like W.H. Lethaby, Halsey Ricardo, J.D. Sedding and C.F.A. Voysey, adopted it.

Some, like Eden Nesfield, E.W. Godwin and, most influential of them all, Norman Shaw, became associated with the "Queen Anne" revival with its similarly un-grandiose approach to building. Truth to materials, simplicity and homeliness were its aims, and the style is characterized by the use of red brick with contrasting white-framed windows or white stone decorations, gabled roofs and bay windows.

The Queen Anne style was found suitable for the apartment blocks that from the 1860s had been seen as a solution to London's housing needs, and for the first garden suburbs, as well as for the substantial houses of well-heeled "aesthetic" families.

This English Domestic Revival, as it became known, was powered by the social and aesthetic philosophies of the Arts and Crafts Movement and was part of a much wider revolution in which design was at last beginning to free itself from historical precedents.

In the work of Voysey can be seen the first stirrings of the Modern Movement, and they were taken a stage further by C.R. Mackintosh in Glasgow. Their work, as well as that of other Arts and Crafts designers such as Morris and Mackmurdo, was the direct inspiration for Art Nouveau on the Continent. This was to be the last thrust of British influence on design for many years.

3
*(3)A view of Antoni Gaudi's unfinished masterpiece, the Sagrada Familia, Barcelona*

# INSPIRATIONS

**1**

*(1) An early 20th-century photograph of the Parthenon, Athens. Greek temples were the inspiration for much Victorian architecture, especially civic buildings such as town halls, libraries and commercial institutions. (3) A photograph of Cologne Cathedral taken in 1887. Continental enthusiasm for the Gothic, never as great as that of the English, was centred on Cologne during the 1840s. The original 13th-century plans for the unfinished cathedral* were discovered in the early 19th century, and in 1842 work began to complete the building according to these designs. Gothic churches were soon being built in both Germany and Austria, while the French, who with some justification claimed to be the originators of Gothic in the first place, were busy studying and recording their medieval buildings under the auspices of a number of newly established archaeological bodies.*

*(2) The title page of A.W.N. Pugin's* The Glossary of Ecclesiastical Ornament and Costume *(1844), an early and fine example of a chromolithographed book. Pugin's many publications as well as his dedication and vast capacity for work made him the most powerful voice in the Gothic revival.*

**2**

**3**

4

5

*Strawberry Hill, the Seat of Mr. Horace Walpole.*

*(4) Pugin's treatise* The True Principles of Pointed or Christian Architecture *(1841) reached a receptive audience, particularly in the emerging generation of religiously fervent architects. Among them, G.E. Street, George Gilbert Scott, George Frederick Bodley and William Butterfield were concerned largely with the building of churches, while William Burges, the most original Gothicist of them all, made his mark equally strikingly on secular buildings. Here, an illustration from Pugin's* An Apology for the Revival of Christian Architecture in England *(1843) illustrates his ideal of ecclesiastical building.*

*(5) One of the most influential of 18th-century "Gothick" adventures was Strawberry Hill, Horace Walpole's house at Twickenham. But whereas the 18th- and early 19th-century Gothick was a decorative style associated with the "picturesque", the Victorian Gothic revival, spearheaded by Pugin, was a carefully researched historical exercise, steeped in religious and moralizing fervour.*

# THE BATTLE OF THE STYLES

(1) Arches at first-floor level around the central hall of the Natural History Museum, London (1873-81). Alfred Waterhouse used shades of yellow and grey terracotta in his dignified evocation of the Romanesque. The round-arched styles of early and pre-Gothic architecture were greatly encourage by Ruskin, but the Classical style was usually preferred for major civic buildings, especially in America. Here Robert Mills's dome on the Capitol, Washington (3), shows the 1830s Grecian at its most impressive.

1

2

3

4

(2) Part of the Portland stone façade of the Law Courts, London, an exercise in Gothic diversity and one of the last great national monuments to be built in the Gothic style. Its architect, the ecclesiological George Edmund Street, died before it was completed in 1882. (4) Design for the west façade of Milan Cathedral, 1887, by the little-known English architect Daniel Brade, a pupil of Paxton. Although his design was not used, it demonstrates the importance of English church architecture in Europe. Both George Gilbert Scott and William Burges made major Gothic contributions across the Channel.

## THE HOUSES OF PARLIAMENT

The Houses of Parliament must be included among the seminal buildings of the Victorian period. Built between 1837 and 1867 by Charles Barry the Classicist and A.W.N. Pugin the Gothicist, it provides a rare fusion of the two styles or, as Pugin himself lamented: "Tudor details on a classic body".

When the competition for the building was launched in 1835, after a fire had destroyed most of the old Palace of Westminster, the Gothic or Elizabethan styles were those prescribed — they were

seen as "British" and therefore more suitable for such an important national institution. Out of 97 entries, 91 were in the Gothic style. Barry's and Pugin's winning contribution, although Classical in its basic plan, was regarded as Gothic, due to Pugin's decoration, both inside and out, in the Perpendicular style. Many of his designs were carried out by the decorating firm of Crace, specialists in the Elizabethan and Gothic styles. Pugin and John Gregory Crace subsequently maintained a close working

relationship.

As well as Pugin's internal architectural details and furnishings the interior decoration included frescoes "of subjects from our national history", for which another national competition had been launched under the aegis of a Royal Commission headed by Prince Albert. The choice of history rather than allegory or mere decorative schemes may have been due to

the example of the Gallery of Victories at Versailles in the 1830s. The use of fresco instead of oil painting was clearly influenced by the fresco-painting School of the ex-Nazarene Peter Cornelius in Dusseldorf. Among the successful artists in the competition were William Dyce, Daniel Maclise, John Tenniel and G.F. Watts, but the project aroused enormous public interest, and large-scale history painting received a fillip.

*(5) Cuthbert Brodrick's palazzo-like design for Leeds Town Hall (1853-58) which, like the contemporaneous St George's Hall, Liverpool, used the Corinthian order for its columned facade. Its urn-topped balustrade as well as the domed clock tower are more reminiscent of the Baroque style than the purely Classical.*

5

# HISTORICAL REVIVALS

(1) *Neuschwanstein Castle in Bavaria (1868-81), a romantic fantasy of fairy-tale Gothic built for King Ludwig of Bavaria. Described by a contemporary French writer as "the only real king of this century", he patronized architects and designers on a lavish scale for his many castles, all of which were highly theatrical recreations of different historical styles. (2) The new opera house in Paris (1874) by Charles Garnier was more extravagantly Baroque than anything produced in the 17th century, its exterior as dramatic as its huge glittering exterior. Garnier went on to design the Casino at Monte Carlo.*

1

2

3

**(4)** *Brockhamptom Church, Herefordshire (1901), by W.R. Lethaby, a stylish essay in the early medieval vernacular.*

*Lethaby was a pupil of Richard Norman Shaw and a vigorous champion of "Arts and Crafts architecture".*

4

**(3)** *Cardiff Castle was designed by William Burges for the Marquess of Bute (1866-81). While the building and most of its decoration is an extravagant and humorous pastiche of medievalism, Burges escaped into an equally colourful Moorish fantasy in the Arab Room in the tower, with its marbled and tiled walls and gilded honeycomb carving. The mosaic coat of arms above the fireplace is that of the Marquess of Bute.* **(5)** *A view of Osborne House, the royal residence on the Isle of Wight (1845-51), designed by Prince Albert and Thomas Cubitt in the form of an Italian Renaissance villa.*

5

# PUBLIC BUILDINGS

(1) The Picture Gallery at the Zwinger Palace, Dresden (1847-9), was the work of the influential German architect Gottfried Semper. He designed buildings in Dresden in a variety of historical styles, and later worked in England (1851-55), notably on sections of the Great Exhibition and as a teacher at Henry Cole's School of Design at Marlborough House, London. His published researches into polychromy in ancient Greek and Roman architecture led to a new approach to colour in building.
(2) The restrained Gothic edifice of Charterhouse School, Surrey (1872), by P.C. Hardwick. One of the most versatile Victorian architects, his other buildings included Euston Station (with his father Philip), The Great Western Hotel, Paddington, and St John's Cathedral, Limerick.

1

2

3

(3) The Midland Grand Hotel, St Pancras (1868-74), was designed by the leading mid-Victorian Gothic revival architect George Gilbert Scott. Although the greater part of his prolific output was concerned with church building or restoration, Scott was also responsible for landmarks such as this and the Albert Memorial.

4

*(4) Battersea Town Hall, South London (1892), by E.W. Mountford. By the 1890s the Baroque form of Classicism was much favoured for public buildings, which often assumed a showy gravitas reminiscent of Sir Christopher Wren. Here white stone and red brick are contrasted in an elaborate but dignified façade complementing E.W. Mountford's Public Library building opposite.*

*(5) Alfred Waterhouse's imposing Gothic façade of the Natural History Museum, London (1873-81), in shades of yellow and grey terracotta. The decoration includes figures of animals and birds both in the stonework and in the iron balustrading of the roof. High Victorian eclecticism (6) can be seen at its most exuberant in W.H. Crossland's Royal Holloway College, Surrey (1879-87). This view of the north courtyard embodies the period's delight in contrasting materials in a daring pastiche of a French Renaissance palace.*

5

6

# MEMORIALS

**(1)** *The Buxton Memorial Fountain, Victoria Tower Gardens, London, was "Erected in 1866 by Charles Buxton MP in commemoration of the Emancipation of Slaves 1834 and in memory of his father Sir T. Fowell Buxton and those associated with him." The design, in stone and marble with mosaic and ceramic decoration, was by Samuel Saunders Teulon.*

2

1

**(2)** *The allegorical figures of Valour and Cowardice on the Wellington Monument in St Paul's Cathedral (1857). The Duke died in 1852 and a competition was held to choose a suitably lofty memorial for a great national hero. Alfred Stevens eventually rose to the occasion with a triumphant Neo-Classical shrine in stone and bronze, which was not, however, finished until 1912, 35 years after his death.*

3

4

5

6

*(3) Asia – one of the white marble groups representing the Continents at the four corners of the Albert Memoriai, designed, like the bronze statue of Prince Albert in the centre, by the sculptor John Henry Foley. The Albert Memorial itself (4) was designed by the Victorians' favourite Gothic architect George Gilbert Scott, who described it as "a colossal statue of the Prince, placed beneath a vast and magnificent shrine or tabernacle and surrounded by works of sculpture illustrating those arts and sciences which he fostered".*

*(5) A marble equestrian piece in the Père-Lachaise cemetery, Paris, commemorating General Gobert, an officer in the Napoleonic army. The sculptor is David d'Angers, 1847. (6) The Gothic canopied monument over Grace Darling's grave in the churchyard at Bamburgh (1846) by C.R. Smith and W.S. Hicks.*

# CIVIC SCULPTURE

(1) The Marsellaise — The Departure of the Volunteers in 1792. *The 12.8m (42ft) stone sculpture from the Arc de Triomphe, Paris (1833-36) by François Rude. French enthusiasm for historical painting and heroic sculpture proved mildly contagious in mid-19th-century Britain and America.* (2) *A painting by Edward Morin, showing the unveiling of the Statue of Liberty in October 1886. This immense symbolic figure, by the French sculptor Frederic-Auguste Bartholdi, with Gustave Eiffel's internal structure, was a gift to the United States from the French nation.*

1

2

4

3

(3) *Thomas Thornycroft's statue of Queen Boadicea driving her chariot, Westminster, London. This ancient "champion of right and might" had a special significance for the myth-loving, empire-building Victorians. Thornycroft spent no less than 15 years working on this, his most famous monument, but it was not erected until 1902.* (4) *John Quincy Adams Ward's bronze monument to Henry Ward Beecher, Cadman Plaza, Brooklyn, New York, 1891. This is a typically romantic presentation of an American hero.*

HENRY WARD BEECHER 1813 1887

**(5)** *Alfred Gilbert's statue of Eros in Piccadilly, London. Gilbert was a leading member of the New School of Sculpture which emerged in the 1860s and also included Alfred Stevens, Frederick Leighton, Hamo Thornycroft and Onslow Ford. Their expressive small-scale sculpture for home decoration made their work popular and commercial, and most of them basked in a succession of prestigious public commissions.*

5

# THE DOMESTIC REVIVAL

1

2

3

**(1)** *Clarendon flats, Balderton Street, Westminster and* **(2)**, *a Victorian terrace typical of thousands built in and around Britain's cities in response to the burgeoning population of the second half of the 19th century.*

**(3)** *Norman Shaw's light touch with revival styles, particularly with the "Queen Anne", established his reputation as the leading architect of the British domestic revival. He built his own house in Ellerdale Road, Hampstead in 1875.*

4

5

(4) Bedford Park, West London, was the first garden suburb, built mainly in the revived Queen Anne style to designs by Norman Shaw and others. The project was the brainchild of Jonathan Carr, a cloth merchant and speculative developer, and in 1881 this leafy and salubrious development was claimed to be "the healthiest place in the world".

(5)This terracotta house in Kensington Court, London, was built in 1885 by Thomas Graham Jackson, a former pupil of George Gilbert Scott. The style is a highly decorated eclectic one, with Gothic, Elizabethan and Queen Anne elements. The initials of the owner, Athelstan Riley, a prominent member of the high-church Oxford Movement, are worked into the decorative borders at first-floor level, and the oriel window on the right is that of his private chapel.

# THE DOMESTIC REVIVAL

Munstead Wood, **(1)**, of which we see the south side, was designed by Edwin Lutyens for his friend, the garden designer Gertrude Jekyll in 1896. It is built in local Surrey stone. Lutyens's early interest in vernacular techniques resulted in some remarkable domestic buildings; later he was to become more famous as a Classical architect.

1

2

**(2)** The south-east corner of The Red House, Bexleyheath, Kent. Philip Webb built this house in 1859-60 for William Morris. Its local materials and unpretentious, Gothic-influenced style heralded the domestic revival of the 1870s.

**(3)** Broadleys (1898-99), overlooking Lake Windermere, is a fine example of C.F.A. Voysey's domestic style. The white rough-cast walls, mullioned windows and wide eaves of this two-storey house are typical, while the triple bay front is an elegant response to the site.

3

4

(4) A New England "Gingerbread Gothic" board-and-batten cottage of the picturesque type favoured by the influential American architect and landscape gardener, Andrew Jackson Downing, whose publications promoted the "civilizing force" of beauty linked with utility in domestic architecture. White Lodge, Wantage (5), was built in 1808-9 by the architect and designer M.H. Baillie Scott who, with Voysey and Mackintosh, did much to promote the English domestic revival on the Continent.

5

(6)The New Jersey residence of George H. Attwood, a characteristically American fusion of the Beaux-Arts style with the picturesque in a wilfully asymmetrical shingle-roofed board-and batten-structure.

6

## JOHN CLAUDIUS LOUDON

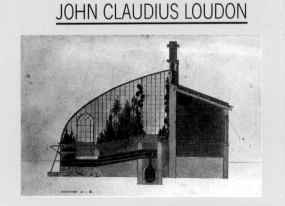

Through his prodigious output of gardening and architectural publications, most notably the *Encyclopaedia of Cottage, Farm and Villa Architecture and Furniture* (1833) Loudon exerted a huge influence on middle-class domestic taste in the early Victorian period. Concerned less with novelty than with practicality, he included designs in the Grecian, Gothic, Elizabethan, "Louis XIV or florid Italian", Indian and Swiss styles, all translated into palatable form for popular use. His own house in Porchester Terrace, London, was the first semi-detached dwelling, and his views on social and educational issues were equally forward-looking. His interest in gardening led him into the realms of glasshouse design, and his invention of ridge-and-furrow construction with curved glazing enabled Paxton and others to construct their glasshouses.

# INDUSTRY AND COMMERCE

*(1)* *These warehouses at Gloucester Docks were built in 1857 in a symmetrical, classically-inspired style, like many utilitarian buildings of the early Victorian period.*

1

2

3

*(2) The Stock Exchange, Amsterdam, built in 1898-1902, is regarded as the masterpiece of H.P. Berlage, who not only* *designed the structure of the brick, metal and glass building but also its interior furnishings and electric lighting.*

*(3) Templeton's carpet factory, Glasgow (1889), by William Leiper was one of the more extravagant examples of a* *commercial building imitating a romantic historical original; in this case, the Doge's Palace in Venice.*

**4**

**(5)**The architect of the gabled and turreted Prudential Assurance Building, Holborn, London, was Alfred Waterhouse, a prolific designer of schools, churches and other public buildings in a range of historicist styles. For many of them, like this and his other famous legacy the Natural History Museum, he favoured the warm tones of terracotta.

**5**

In F.J. Ward's Albert Buildings, Queen Victoria Street, London **(4)**, various forms of Gothic arcading with bold cornices provide a distinguished solution to a difficult corner site. Built in 1869, this is one of the City of London's last remaining Victorian commercial buildings. The Monadnock Block, Chicago **(6)** was one of the last skyscrapers to be built without a steel frame construction. It was built in 1889-91 and designed by the partnership of Burnham & Root, who also conceived the Masonic Temple (1891) of 22 storeys, built on a steel skeleton — the tallest building in the world at that time.

# CHAPTER TWO
# TRANSPORT AND INVENTION

**(1)** *Otto Wagner's iron-vaulted entrance to the Karlsplatz Station in Vienna (1897-99). Wagner's rationalist approach to architecture — "Nothing that is not practical can be beautiful" — grew out of the Arts and Crafts movement and was an important influence on the development of the modern movement with its overt use of modern constructional techniques.*

The course of design in the 19th century was to a large extent determined by the engineers — the chief technicians in a technocratic age — and of all their achievements the development of steam locomotion was most crucial. It had a revolutionary effect on transport both on land and by sea and therefore on commercial and social life throughout the world. Caught up in the steam revolution were bridge- and canal-building projects, land-drainage schemes, lighthouses, ship-building, and the huge network of railways whose architecture made its impact on the countryside all over Europe and North America.

The designers of these structures — Thomas Telford, George and Robert Stephenson, James Rennie, Isambard Kingdom Brunel, William Fairbairn, Henry Bessemer, Ferdinand de Lesseps and many others — sometimes achieved bold visual statements in their use of new materials and construction techniques. Yet very often, and increasingly as the century wore on, they were constrained by traditional precedents and fashions.

Iron suspension bridges had to be built with Gothic towers for uprights; railway buildings pretended to be Classical temples or medieval castles; factory chimneys were shaped like Chinese pagodas and warehouses were made to look like Venetian palaces. In many instances the architect's real role was to mask the work of the engineer.

### The railways

The first public steam railway was the Stockton & Darlington, surveyed and built by George Stephenson and opened in 1825. It was soon followed by others: the Liverpool & Manchester Railway, the first section of the St Etienne to Lyons Railway and the first 13 miles of the Baltimore & Ohio Railroad were all opened in 1830.

New railways and the locomotives and rolling stock for them became a major engineering focus during the 1830s all over Europe as far as Russia, and in America, but the real boom in railway development came in the 1840s, with all its spin-offs in commercial and social life. America's Union Pacific Railroad linked up with the Central Pacific Railroad in 1869 to form the world's first trans-continental railway.

The introduction of underground railways as a means of easing congestion and to link the main-line termini of cities began in 1863 with the opening of London's Metropolitan Railway. This was carried just below the surface of the streets and was serviced by the latest in locomotive technology — condensing engines which consumed their own steam, developed by Daniel Gooch, Locomotive Superintendent of the Great Western Railway. To the Metropolitan were soon added the District and later the Circle lines, which together provided a subterranean network all over London and to its periphery.

The first deep-level "tube" trains, operated by electric traction, were introduced in 1890 in the City & South London Railway. Benefiting from the pioneering work of the London underground, other systems began in Glasgow (1896), Paris (1900) and New York (1905).

### By road and sea

At the beginning of the period, the stage coach provided the chief method of public transport, and horse-drawn vehicles supplied most social, agricultural and commercial needs. By the end of the 19th century, both the railways and the new petrol-engined cars and buses were becoming normal passenger vehicles. Electric-powered trams replaced horse-drawn omnibuses in some towns, while the bicycle had evolved from a machine of bone-shaking adventure to one of pneumatic-tyred safety, fit even for a lady to ride. Thanks to the 18th- and 19th-century road-building schemes of engineers such as General Wade (in Scotland), Metcalf, MacAdam and Telford, roads had been much improved by this time.

Sea travel also changed dramatically in the middle of the 19th century. Wooden sailing ships continued to ply their way across the Atlantic, typically bringing a cargo of timber to Europe and returning with emigrants from Scotland or Ireland, housed in miserably uncomfortable and overcrowded conditions. The well-heeled could travel in relative comfort in the "packet" steam boats which by mid-century were making regular and speedy trips to and from America, many of them subsidized by the mail they carried.

Iron was now being used to build passenger ships powered either by steam alone or by a more economic theatre to be electrically lit was the Savoy in 1887, and electric street lights did not appear until 1891.

The domestic use of electricity was just one of a whole range of late 19th-century scientific and technical advances that impinged on everyday life of rich and poor alike. The most far-reaching were probably the telephone, invented by Alexander Graham Bell, the phonograph (and the electric light bulb) by Thomas Alva Edison, wireless telegraphy by Guglielmo Marconi and the cinematograph by the Lumière brothers. The apparatus for all these, plus useful inventions like typewriters, sewing machines, vacuum cleaners and portable cameras, constituted an inexhaustible challenge to the designer.

*(2) An advertisement of about 1900 extolling the wonders of the new electric light, and (3) a Moya Visible model No. 2 Typewriter with original type sleeve and three-row keyboard. The typewriter was just one of the many Victorian inventions we now take for granted. Others include the telephone, the vacuum cleaner, the washing machine and even the electric dishwasher.*

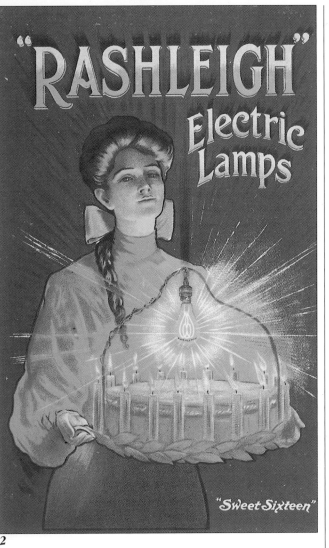

"RASHLEIGH" Electric Lamps

"Sweet Sixteen"

2

combination of steam and sail. The relative inefficiency of early steam engines and their need for huge stocks of coal (and the consequent loss of cargo space) meant that steam alone was neither possible nor economic for the long-haul routes to Australasia and India until much later.

Comfort was becoming a commercially marketable asset, and passenger ships had as much attention lavished on their interior fittings and facilities as on their engineering and structure. Separate dining saloons, libraries, smoking rooms and other amenities now replaced the single communal room of early passenger ships, while running water, ventilation and refrigeration were provided on long routes.

### The age of electricity
Electric light was quite usual in these big liners from the early 1880s onward, although ashore the first British

3

# THE EXHIBITIONS

1

2

3

(1) This picture of the interior of the transept, carefully designed to accommodate mature trees, gives an idea of the vast scale of Paxton's Crystal Palace, to which more than six million people flocked for the Great Exhibition, held from May to October, 1851.

(2) A view of the Crystal Palace from the south side. Its construction included 293,655 panes of glass and 24 miles of guttering. Dostoevski wrote that it was "like a biblical picture, something out of Babylon, a prophecy ... coming to pass before your eyes."

*(4) The frontispiece of the Catalogue of the Great Exhibition, produced by* The Art Journal.

## PRINCE ALBERT

The young Prince Albert, who married Queen Victoria in 1840, was handsome, clever and imbued with a deep sense of public duty. He was immediately and hugely popular. Through his tireless public works, active patronage and personal talents he had a profound effect on the arts of the Victorian period. He worked for the improvement of living conditions for the poor; he chaired the Royal Commission on the rebuilding of the Houses of Parliament, and from 1843 he was president of the Royal Society of Arts. This led to his close collaboration with the dynamic Henry Cole, whose whole life was devoted to the improvement of national design and who became the first director of the South Kensington Museum, later the Victoria & Albert. Their plans for a series of exhibitions for "the encouragement of the application of art to practical purposes" progressed into the Great Exhibition of 1851.

The medal of St George shown here was one of the awards at the Great Exhibition. It was designed in 1851 by William Wyon, whose head of Queen Victoria had already been immortalized in the Penny Black stamp, first issued in 1840.

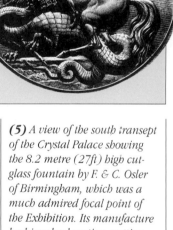

*(3) A potlid showing the Paris Exposition Universelle of 1867 "arranged in concentric bands, with a garden in the middle". The designer was Gustave Eiffel, who was to produce the Eiffel Tower for the 1889 Exposition Tricoulere, held to celebrate the centenary of the French Revolution.*

*(5) A view of the south transept of the Crystal Palace showing the 8.2 metre (27ft) high cut-glass fountain by F. & C. Osler of Birmingham, which was a much admired focal point of the Exhibition. Its manufacture had involved casting, cutting and polishing no less than four tons of glass.*

# GLASS AND METAL

1

2

*(1) The Palm House at Kew Gardens (1844-48) was a collaboration between the architect Decimus Burton and the Dublin engineer Richard Turner. Arched metal frames support curved glass panels set in mullions with wrought-iron ribs. (2) The Dittenhoffer Building, New York, built in 1870 by T.R. Jackson, is an example of the use of cast iron in an Italian Renaissance style. In many of the new arcades, railway stations and markets, such as Smithfield, London (3), wrought-iron girders (strong under tension) were used for such parts as arched spans, while supporting pillars, decorative details and additions like lamps were of cast iron (strong in compression but brittle under tension).*

3

*(4) The Forth railway suspension bridge (1883-90) designed by Sir John Fowler, Sir Benjamin Baker and others, was one of the earliest steel structures in Britain and a rare use of a new material in undisguised form. By the 1870s steel had become available in large quantities through the development of Sir Henry Bessemer's conversion process (1857), but it was not widely used in Britain until the turn of the century.*

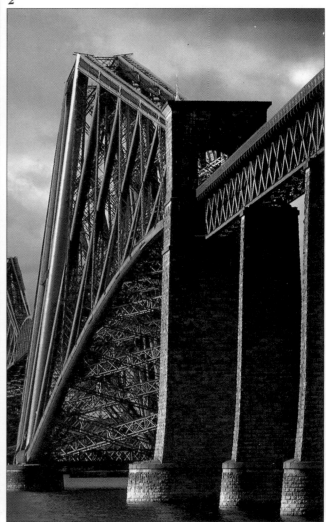

4

5

6

7

(5) The Eiffel Tower, the tallest structure of its time at 250m (984ft), was erected for the Paris Exhibition of 1889. Four iron pylons flow into a single column of fretted metalwork. It is the most famous monument of the bridge-building engineer Gustave Eiffel, whose other feats include the iron interior of the Statue of Liberty, New York, and the Garabit Viaduct in France, made of huge arches and trussed beams in preformed sections.

(6) The southern entrance to the transept of the Crystal Palace. Work on the building began in July 1850, when stakes were driven into the ground to indicate the position of the columns. As each cast girder arrived it was rigorously tested for load-bearing capacity by means of a special machine, and stacked ready for use. The Paxton gutters and sash-bars were prepared in mile lengths. sash-bars were prepared by mile lengths.

(7) The dramatic wide-curving iron arches of Central Station, York (1871-77), by William Peachy and Thomas Prosser, are among the most pleasing achievements of Victorian railway architecture.

# ROAD TRANSPORT

*1*

**(1)** *Two adventurous ladies taking the air in 1895 in a car by the Frenchmen René Panhard and Emile Levassor, who were the first to install the engine under a hood at the front of the car. Horse-drawn carriages* **(2)***, however, remained the most usual genteel transport until the end of the century. This is a landau of the 1880s.*

*2*

**(3)** *Walter Hancock's four-wheeled steam coaches were the first self-propelled road vehicles to run on a scheduled passenger service. Between 1831 and 1840, they plied the route from Stratford in Essex to London, reaching speeds of up to 15 miles per hour.*

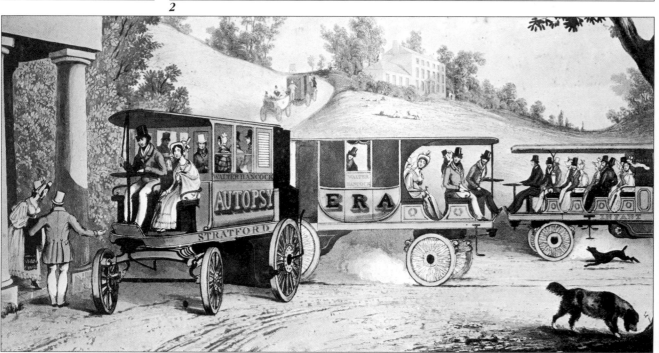

*3*

4

5

6

7

*(4) Horse-drawn goods and passenger vehicles of all descriptions crowding across London Bridge in the late 19th century. The speed of transport may have been slower, but traffic jams and accidents were as much a hazard of city life as they are today.*

*(5)A print by Currier & Ives showing fashionable turnouts in Central Park, New York. They include a brougham (top left) and a barouche (right). (6) The first horseless carriage produced by Henry Ford (1892). Later he was to build the American car industry and make an immense personal fortune.*

*(7)The first vis-a-vis of de Dion Bouton, 1899. The association between the Comte de Dion and Georges Bouton began in 1883; at first they designed steam road vehicles, but from 1895 they developed a new type of gasoline-engined vehicle, tiny, light and speedy, with a rear engine and handlebar steering.*

# THE RAILWAYS

(1) *The interior of a carriage on the Rock Island Railroad which ran between San Francisco and New York, c. 1875. The upholstered seats could be transformed into beds for night-time travelling.*

(2) *"Across the Continent: Westward the Course of Empire Takes its Way" — a Currier & Ives lithograph of 1868 depicting a steam train travelling through an American outback village.*

1

2

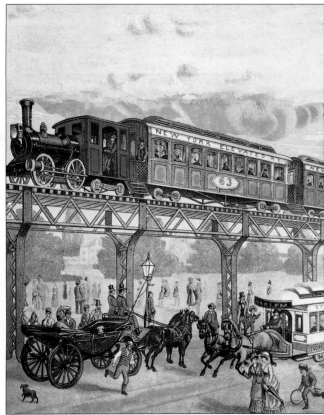

4

3

(3) *The New York Elevated railway, an attempt to ease congestion in the city, was opened in 1872. So successful was it that the New York subway was a relatively late development.* (4) *A locomotive of the Great Western Railway, 1846, designed by Daniel Gooch and made at the GWR's works at Swindon. This line, originally conceived as a link between London and Bristol, was developed to cover the whole of Wales and south-west England. Its first engineer, Isambard Kingdom Brunel, favoured the broad gauge (7ft), which gave a comfortable spaciousness to the carriages and set the GWR apart from its contemporaries until the standard gauge was introduced from 1869 to 1892.*

## PULLMAN COMFORT

Long coaches with a central aisle and open seating first appeared in Austria and France in the 1840s, and corridor trains were introduced in the 1890s. As with hotels, it was America who gave the lead in railway comfort. George Mortimer Pullman, founder of the Pullman Palace Car Company, Illinois, in 1867, invented a new type of railway coach modelled on the comfortable cabins of American steamboats. The picture shows the interior of a Pullman smoking car on the Southern Pacific Railroad, *circa* 1900. American trains had sleeping cars, dining cars and lavatories long before they were introduced in Europe, and some of Pullman's trains even offered showers, barbers' shops and office compartments complete with the services of stenographers.

*(5)An electric locomotive pulling a steam train on the Baltimore & Ohio Railroad, c. 1895. A four-mile tunnel section under Baltimore was electrified and the steam trains were pulled through it to avoid the nuisance of smoke and noise in the city.*

5

6

7

*This Currier & Ives print (6) shows "The Lightning Express" trains (1863) with their huge funnels and apron fronts (known as cow-catchers) for clearing cattle or snow off the line. These designs are typical of American locomotives in the period following the Civil War (7). American railroad companies prided themselves on the good food and elegant comfort of their dining cars.*

# RIVER AND SEA

(1) *Isambard Kingdom Brunel's* Great Britain, *at 3,270 tons, was the first big iron ship and the first large vessel to be driven by a screw propeller. Built between 1839 and 1843,* she ran aground on the Irish coast in 1846, but her iron hull withstood nearly a year's battering by the sea and she was eventually refloated. She served on the Australia route for 23 years, carried troops to the Crimea, and to India during the Mutiny, and was used, without her engines, as a sailing boat in the 1880s.*

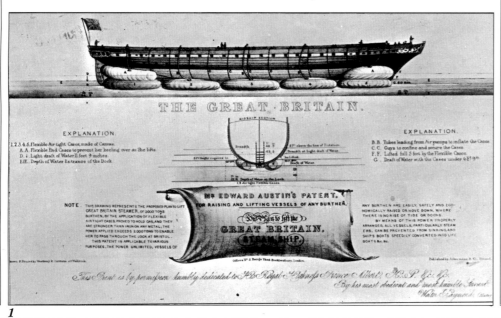

1

## THE ATLANTIC CROSSING

The earliest steam vessels were paddle-propelled, a method not well suited to the rough seas on ocean voyages, but good for short coastal journeys around Britain and ideal for navigation in shallow waters such as America's lakes and rivers. But steam power was not to be so limited, and as early as 1838 a transatlantic passenger service was inaugurated with *Sirius* and with the first of Brunel's three great steamships, *Great Western*. His second, the screw-driven *Great Britain*, marked the next stage in steamship development.

The first regular transatlantic steamship line was founded by the Canadian Samuel Cunard. He had four steam-driven, paddle-propelled ships built on the Clyde and the first was *Britannia* (above). She made her maiden voyage in 1840 and two years later Charles Dickens sailed in her.

It was the coming together of three major factors that allowed steamship development to reach the success it was to enjoy by the 1870s. First was the production of iron plates large enough to enable these vast metal hulls to be built. This in its turn provided a suitable housing for the ship's screw. The third and most important development was the compound engine. By the 1860s this provided a much more efficient and therefore economical way to drive the screw.

2

(2) *An early photograph of The Eddystone Lighthouse, designed by the Trinity House engineer James N. Douglass and first lit in May 1882. It was the fourth lighthouse on this notoriously hazardous rocky reef off the Devon coast, and like other rock towers presented appalling difficulties for engineers and builders.*

(3) *The comfortably appointed main cabin of the Mississippi steamboat* J.M. White. *It was interiors such as this that provided the models for George Mortimer Pullman's luxurious railway carriages.*

(4) *Steamboats were used on American waterways long before the advent of the railways, and they continued all through the 19th century. The subject of this Currier & Ives lithograph is the* Mayflower, *a Mississippi steamboat of 1855.*

*3*

*4*

(5) *The lavish dining room of the* Lucania *was designed in what was described as "the modified Italian style", complete with aspidistras and 430 velvet-covered swivelling armchairs. The white and gold coffered ceiling is supported by Ionic columns, and the wall panelling is of carved Spanish mahogany. The* Lucania *was one of Cunard's travelling palaces on the North Atlantic route in the 1890s.*

51

*5*

# THE RISE OF INDUSTRY

(1) Steam power was crucial to Victorian industrial progress: here the great Corliss steam engine is being celebrated at the Philadelphia Centennial Exhibition in 1876. (2) The agricultural machinery producer Bellaire Manufacturing Company, Ohio, was typical of many sited close both to rail and water transport. Increasing mechanization of processes, in this case (3) calico printing, made many products more widely accessible, but designers were not always successful in adapting to mass-production. Schemes run by organizations like the Art Union and the establishment of Government schools of design were attempts to improve design for industry.

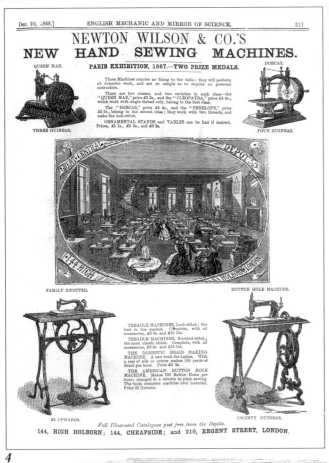

**4**

**5**

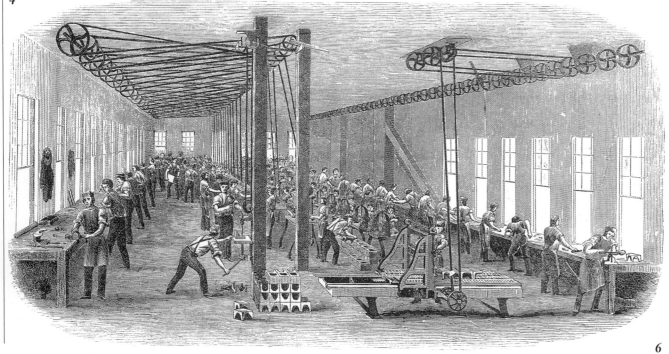

**6**

*(4, 5, 6) Although various inventors in Europe developed sewing machines in the first half of the 19th century, it was in America that the most successful developments took place. The first practical domestic sewing machine was patented by Isaac Merritt Singer in 1851, and his products, "simple, strong, speedy", were to dominate the English as well as the American market for many years. The example above is a Grover & Baker machine, c. 1873.*

One of a pair of carved and
upholstered walnut chairs made by
the New York firm of Pottier & Stymms
in 1875 and exhibited at the
Philadelphia Centennial Exhibition of
1876. The style of decoration is
predominantly Renaissance (with an
uncomfortable mask in the small of
the back!) but the carving of the front
rail can only be described as
"aesthetic".

# CHAPTER THREE
# FURNITURE AND INTERIORS

**1**

*(1) A photograph, probably dating from the 1890s, of the drawing room in the Stanford White residence, New York City. This exuberant, money-no-object mélange includes Baroque, Rococo, Neo-Classical and Renaissance decoration, with furniture in a corresponding hotch-potch of styles. The Classical bronzes and the 17th-century paintings reflect the prevailing passion for collecting among the well-to-do, and indeed, architectural features like the fireplaces and the ceiling mouldings were probably acquired abroad.*

Although traditionally — and misleadingly — 1830 has been regarded as the cut-off point between hand-crafted and machine-made furniture, the process of mechanization in the furniture industry was actually much more gradual. Hand-work continued to be used throughout the century for certain processes.

Furniture finishing was the earliest to be affected by mechanization, and machine-cut veneers and mechanical carving account for much of the over-loaded surface decoration of the early Victorian period. As the century wore on, production became more adjusted to mechanical means, and mass-production methods had to be introduced simply to keep pace with the demands of a rapidly expanding population.

The introduction of the coiled spring in the late 1820s led to the characteristic weighty contours and deep buttoning of Victorian seat furniture. The growing use of spirit varnishes, or French polish, begun during the Regency period, gave furniture a mirror-like "piano" finish unlike the mellow shine previously achieved with beeswax and turpentine and, incidentally, resulted in a great deal of 18th-century furniture being quite unsuitably repolished by the Victorians.

Painted simulations such as graining and marbling were extremely popular finishes during the 1850s and 1860s, but went out of fashion by the 1870s. By the last decades of the century, staining and ebonizing enjoyed a renewed vogue. The well-established American tradition for painted or stencilled furniture was maintained in the "fancy" chairs of Lambert Hitchcock and others working in the eastern states at least until mid-century.

### Historical styles

Styles largely followed those laid down by architects, and indeed many of the period's designers of buildings made their mark as strongly inside them as without. Among the first was Pugin, with his radically Gothic furniture, but many others followed.

While high-minded and romantically inclined Victorians lived in thickly upholstered opulence amid castellated bookcases or crocketed cabinets, and sat on Gothic-arched chairs at tables supported on clustered columns, the more worldly majority followed the conservative line of classically inspired revivalism.

Much mid-19th-century furniture was influenced, as it had been since time immemorial, by France, whose Beaux-Arts style found favour with a newly prosperous middle class all over Europe and America, bent on showing off its wealth as ostentatiously as possible.

The sort of furniture illustrated in J.C. Loudon's *Encyclopaedia of Cottage, Farm and Villa Architecture and Furniture* (1833, several re-issues) probably represented the taste of the majority more accurately than any other design book. Loudon included designs in the Gothic and Elizabethan styles; interestingly, with regard to the latter, he did not hesitate to recommend the "making up" of furniture from genuine Elizabethan fragments which were then abundantly available. His "Grecian" designs were descended from those of Thomas Hope and his Regency followers, but their carved embellishment and Rococo-inspired scrolls and curlicues, undisciplined acanthus leaves and naturalistic florets would have appalled the earlier purists.

Even Loudon himself decried the current attention to decoration at the expense of unity in furniture. The aim of the average customer was, he said, "to get a display of rich workmanship, at as cheap a rate as possible".

### The Great Exhibition

The Great Exhibition of 1851 included furniture in all the extremes that could be dreamed up by manufacturers bent on novelty and extravagant effects but with little regard for suitability. Indeed, the jury of the furniture section commented that "articles of furniture are too often crowded with unnecessary embellishment, which, besides adding to their cost, interferes with their use, purpose and convenience."

While most everyday furniture of the time followed

**2**

For him, as for others, the answer seemed to lie in the medieval period, but whereas Pugin had associated the Gothic with spiritual purity, Morris looked to it for honesty of craftsmanship and integrity of design with function. Pugin's archaeological approach gave way to an entirely original interpretation of the medieval by Morris and his followers.

The architects William Burges and Norman Shaw, Gothicists *par excellence,* were already producing their powerfully structural and brightly painted 13th-century-inspired versions of the medieval in refreshing contrast to the stifling excesses of Victorian eclecticism.

The design principles – if not the philosophy – of the Arts and Crafts campaigners soon filtered through to the large furniture-producing companies such as Holland & Son, Jackson & Graham, Collinson & Lock, and Gillow, who found an eager market for the new "art" furniture and employed eminent designers such as Bruce Talbert, E.W. Godwin and T.E. Collcutt. They were encouraged by the success of Talbert's *Gothic Forms Applied to Furniture, Metal Work and Decoration for Domestic Purposes* and Charles Locke Eastlake's *Hints on Household Taste,* both published in 1868.

### Reproduction furniture

All through the Victorian period, the making of reproductions and copies of earlier styles provided the bread and butter of manufacturers on both sides of the Atlantic. The

*(2) A mid-19th-century walnut davenport, a usefully small type of desk that had existed since the 1790s, and was to prove exceedingly popular with the Victorians. This example shows the curly-figured walnut that gradually became preferred to the smart dark severity of rosewood in cabinet-making. Mahogany continued to be much used, while oak was chosen for Gothic and Renaissance furniture as well as by the vernacular revivalists and by country craftsmen. (3) Detail of a side table made by Herter Brothers, c. 1882. This is a typical piece of "art" furniture, with an inlaid motif of stylized flowers and leaves that owes much to Japan.*

various historicist styles in watered-down form, most of it showed more regard for comfort than the pieces exhibited at the Great Exhibition. Relatively simple furniture of good quality, mostly deriving from Regency types, was still favoured by the less extrovert, but it looked very different arranged in the cluttered informality that characterized the Victorian interior.

In the years following the Great Exhibition, design books purveying favourite historical styles were published. The first was Blackie's *Cabinet Maker's Assistant* (1853), much used by provincial makers working in Elizabethan and "Louis" modes. *The Cabinet of Practical, Useful and Decorative Furniture Designs* (1856) by Henry Lawford had designs for French marquetry and boulle work as well as for Elizabethan, Gothic and Rococo furniture. The most elaborate designs were in John Braund's *Illustrations of Furniture* (1858).

### Functional design

William Morris strongly disapproved of the displays at the Great Exhibition, describing them as "wonderfully ugly", and he it was who led the inevitable reaction away from the "stuffy inconvenience" of current furnishings and towards a new simplicity.

**3**

*(1) The Saville chair of c. 1880, by George Jack, the New York-born architect and designer who became Philip Webb's chief assistant and later the principal furniture designer for Morris & Co. The chair is upholstered in Morris's "Honeycomb" fabric.*

*(2) Production No.13, a cane-seated chair of bent beechwood by Michael Thonet of Vienna. Thonet was the world's first manufacturer of mass-produced knock-down furniture. Designs like this, first made in the 1850s, must have seemed astoundingly avant-garde at the time, but the cheapness of his chairs ensured their success and they found their way all over the world in their thousands.*

**1**

furniture embellished with sunflowers, chrysanthemums, peacocks, sunbursts and other "Japanese" motifs, or carved with "oriental" fretwork. The use of turned spindles and bamboo brought a new lightness into furniture, and painted flowery panels, inset tiles, or incised and gilded patterns gave colour.

Firms like Shoolbred, Smee, Collinson & Lock, William Watts, Marsh, Jones & Cribb and others ensured that the homes of the middle classes were well supplied with fashionably "aesthetic" furniture, which at first was often of good quality and careful design; but the debasing of this style through the untrammelled mass-commercialization of the 1890s ensured its eventual downfall.

### Furnishing textiles and wallpaper

The eclectic architecture and furniture of the 1840s and 1850s were complemented by textiles and wallpapers of

wealthy, led by the Queen, procured slavishly precise copies of 18th-century furniture, sometimes from Parisian craftsmen but also, increasingly, from others based in London.

Firms like John Webb, Wright & Mansfield and Edwards & Roberts were celebrated for the high quality of their reproductions of French furniture, while English styles such as Chippendale, "Adam", Hepplewhite and, by the end of the century, Sheraton, were widely purveyed as "thoroughly national". ("Queen Anne" was the label attached to almost any style vaguely reminiscent of the earlier 18th century.) Even Morris & Co. established a secure line in "Georgian" furniture in the 1890s.

### The Japanese taste

The re-opening of trade with Japan in the 1860s had a tremendous impact both in Europe and America, and in particular affected the design and development of "aesthetic" furniture in the 1870s and 1880s. Designers such as E.W. Godwin, Christopher Dresser, Lewis F. Day, Thomas Jeckyll and T.E. Collcutt inspired a whole generation of mass-produced — and sometimes ridiculed —

**2**

similarly confusing exuberance: gilded Rococo *boiseries* flourished in Renaissance splendour; *trompe-l'oeil* Gothic arches clambered in illogical three-dimensional patterns up walls framed with "olden time" carved woodwork, and the most formal "Louis" schemes were garlanded with naturalistic blossoms.

On both sides of the Atlantic, flowers bloomed most successfully, and if some of the roses were a little overblown in the second half of the century, at least their new aniline colours lightened the gloom of over-festooned windows and the oppressive surfeit of furniture.

For the Victorians, comfort was achieved with upholstery and opulence with patterning and draped fabrics: the more of each one could cram into a room, the more pleasing the effect. Curtains were hung in great swags; chair coverings were flounced and fringed; tables and pianos were draped and mantelpieces frilled.

Favourite colours included maroon, purple and mossy green, all of which were translated into thick velvets and lustrous damasks for both upholstery and curtaining. Even for those whose idea of comfort included light and space or who, less intent on opulent effects, lived with old-fashioned Regency furniture alongside the latest Elizabethan or Rococo revivals, the patterns of carpets, curtains and wallpapers were a happy hotch-potch.

The move towards stronger colours from the 1830s onward was largely inspired by research into the use of polychrome decoration in the ancient world — hitherto imagined as a marble whiteness — by the Franco-German architect-designers Jacques-Ignace Hittorf and Gottfried Semper. Their publications and important decorative schemes in France and Germany spread their influence. Semper worked in London for several years, designing furniture and decoration and teaching in Henry Cole's School of Design at Marlborough House. Owen Jones led the English revival in polychromy, and his *Grammar of Ornament* (1856) was the culmination of many years study, of the use of colour in early civilizations and of the patterns of other cultures.

Of particular importance during the last two decades were the Silver Studios, founded in 1880 by Arthur Silver. The firm's designs for wallpaper, textiles, linoleum, metalwork and printing were purveyed through a number of retailers to an increasingly discerning public. Their Art Nouveau productions of the 1890s were exported all over Europe and to America, and Arthur Silver's revival of stencilling, for wall decoration and fabrics, was widely copied.

### Embroidery and Tapestry

An artistic movement to revive ecclesiastical needlework was promoted as part of the Gothic revival by the architects Pugin and Street. In 1854 Street founded the Ladies' Ecclesiastical Embroidery Society and others followed. Vestments designed by various architects were worked, mainly in the medieval applied technique.

The interest in this revival of needlework artistry was given a secular dimension by William Morris, who, in the 1860s, began to design embroideries for the Red House. Helped by his family, he explored old techniques such as crewelwork, producing hangings and coverlets with medieval-inspired subjects, or with his unmistakable flowing plant compositions in naturally dyed wools or silks on linen.

The Victorians' love of strong colours and sentimental narrative was well served by the garish Berlin woolwork that had gathered popularity since it was first introduced from Germany in the early 19th century. Designs printed on squared paper, with the canvas and wools for working them, were sold by the "fancy" retailers such as Wilks's Warehouse in Regent Street.

From the late 1850s, when aniline dyes came into use, the wool colours were more brilliant than ever, and by this time canvas could be purchased ready prepared with the design. Biblical scenes or evocations of "olden time", particularly those inspired by Sir Walter Scott's novels, paintings by Landseer or Winterhalter and sentimental pictures of children and animals, were among the favourite subjects, but flowers were overwhelmingly popular.

*(3) A Victorian triple-seated "conversation" settee or "sociable" of the type popular in the mid-19th century. Although the gilded woodwork is in the Neo-Classical style, the deep-buttoned upholstery and convoluted S-shaped design proclaims its Victorian-ness.*

# INSPIRATIONS

**(1)** *An early 17th-century oak panel, carved, painted and gilded. Strapwork patterns such as this were widely adopted for the Victorian neo-Renaissance designs.*

**(2)** *An American Shaker rocking chair in cherrywood, c. 1815-20. William Morris's commitment to functional design and his aversion to useless ornament seems to echo the philosophy of the Shakers.*

*For them, beauty could only exist in the useful, and in their concentration on function, proportion and purity of line they produced some of the most enduringly graceful furniture ever made.*

**3**

**4**

**5**

*(4) Persian patterns from Owen Jones's* Grammar of Ornament *(1856), embodying his principles of design (for example, "All ornament should be based upon a geometrical construction") as well as providing a fund of ideas and motifs for artists and craftsmen in every field. Jones's influence also helped to promote the use of colour on furniture from the 1860s onwards.*

*(3) A late 17th-century French cabinet decorated in Boulle marquetry in pewter and brass on a tortoiseshell ground, with gilt bronze mounts. Reproductions and copies of ornate French furniture from this and later periods were made by firms such as Holland & Son, Jackson & Graham, Wright & Mansfield, Edwards & Roberts, and Hindley & Wilkinson. Some were of high quality, claiming to be "not surpassed even in Paris".*

*(5) A marble-topped side table of carved and gilded wood from the Amalienburg Pavilion, Schloss Nymphenburg, Bavaria (1739). François de Cuvilliés's designs are among the most exuberant of all Rococo adventures, and many of their decorative elements found their way on to Victorian furniture and objects.*

# THE MEDIEVALISTS

*(1) The "Philosophy" cabinet, designed by William Burges in 1879 for the Golden Chamber at his own Tower House, Melbury Road, London. A wardrobe made in the form of a battlemented tower, it is painted and gilded with figures and scenes depicting the domestic troubles of philosophers and literary men. The lower half of the cabinet is decorated with medieval ornament on a parchment-coloured background, while domestic animals play below.*

*(2) A pair of carved oak X-frame side chairs with Gothic tracery in the backs, designed by A.W.N. Pugin, and (3) an oak sideboard in the Gothic style associated with Eastlake and Talbert. The diagonal panelling of the side doors and the panels of low-relief carving on the spandrels of the mirror are typical of the 1870s.*

1

2

3

(4) A design for a bookcase (1835) by A.W.N. Pugin, the chief propagandist of the Victorian Gothic revival. During the 1850s and 60s, under the influence of Ruskin, Pugin's Perpendicular Gothic of the 1830s and 40s gave way to the round-arched forms of the 13th century. (5) The Medieval Court at the Great Exhibition with its mixture of church and domestic furnishings, many of them designed by Pugin. The setting was largely by William Burges.

5

Book Case

6

(6) William Burges's witty design for a fireplace at Cardiff Castle (1868-81), which he transformed into a brilliant medieval fantasy for the Marquess of Bute. Burges designed the stained glass, sculpture, ceramics, tiles, heraldic decoration and murals as well as the architectural features.

# ECLECTICISM

**(1)** *The Great Bed at Scotney Castle, a fine example of the mid-19th-century "Tudorbethan" style, and* **(2)** *a piano made by Gillow of Lancaster and London, possibly to the design of B.J. Talbert. His* Gothic Forms Applied to Furniture, Metal Work and Decoration for Domestic Purposes *was published in 1868, and its sequel,* Examples of Ancient and Modern Furniture, Metal Work, Tapestries, Decorations *in 1876. He is regarded as one of the most accomplished commercial interpreters of both the reformed Gothic and the "Artistic" styles, both of which are exemplified by this piano. He provided furniture designs for Holland & Sons and Jackson & Graham of London, and Marsh, Jones & Cribb of Leeds, as well as Gillow.*

2

1

**(3)** *An oak table with an octagonal top in the simplified Gothic style advocated by C.L. Eastlake in* Hints on Household Taste *(1868).*

3

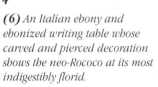

**(4)** A carved and turned mahogany chair in the "Jacobethan" style of the mid-19th century, with Berlin woolwork upholstery, and **(5)** an oak sideboard carved "in the Renaissance style, with much taste and spirit". This elaborate mixture of strapwork, acanthus leaves, lion masks, draped swags and urns was exhibited in the Great Exhibition by "Mr T.W. Caldecott, of London".

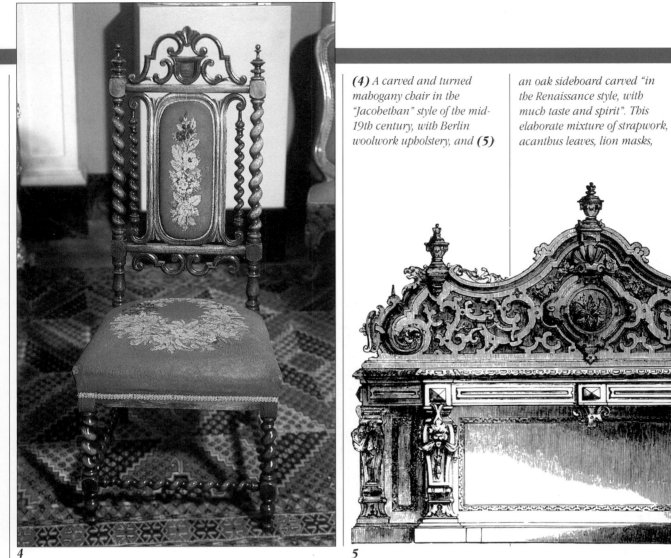

4

5

**(6)** An Italian ebony and ebonized writing table whose carved and pierced decoration shows the neo-Rococo at its most indigestibly florid.

**(7)** One of a set of carved mahogany chairs in the elaborate pseudo-George III style typical of the late 19th century.

6

7

# INTERIORS

(1) The ornate and upholstered grandeur of the neo-Rococo can be seen in this American interior of the mid-19th century, with elaborately carved furniture by John Henry Belter. (2) A corner of the Arab Hall, Leighton House, built 1877-79 by George Aitchison for Frederick Leighton, later to become President of the Royal Academy. To this exotic Moorish pastiche, which became a social Mecca for the artistic élite of the period, William de Morgan contributed tiles, Walter Crane the mosaic frieze and Randolph Caldecott the capitals of the columns.

1

(3) The Victorian tendency to mix colours and styles indiscriminately is captured in this eclectic interior. A deep-buttoned "sociable" or "tête-à-tête" sits in front of a Neo-Classical chimney with a gilded French bergère and a painted English Chippendale-style armchair in the background.

2

3

**4**

*(4) The full-blown Gothic revival can be seen in the drawing room of Eastnor Castle, Herefordshire, remodelled by Augustus Pugin in the 1840s. The fan vaulting, fireplace, table, sideboard and chairs are all to his design; the chandelier was copied from an example in Nuremberg. The castle itself is a sham Gothic pile dating from 1812-15 and designed by Sir Robert Smirke, architect of the British Museum, London.*

# INTERIORS

(1) *Detail of the studio wall mirror in Victor Horta's house in Brussels, 1898. The Belgian architect and designer is regarded as one of the chief pioneers of the Art Nouveau style. The characteristic whiplash tendrils to be seen here were widely copied.*

1

2

(2) *This magazine illustration of the parlour of Abraham Lincoln's House, Springfield, Illinois (1860) shows a surprisingly uncluttered but otherwise typical middle-class room of the mid-19th century.*
(3) *Whistler's astonishing Peacock Room (1876-77) was the dining room at 49 Prince's Gate, London, the home of the shipping magnate Francis Leyland. Originally designed by Thomas Jeckyll, the room housed Leyland's collection of Chinese blue and white porcelain against a background of antique Spanish leather, as well as a portrait by Whistler. The artist was commissioned to make some small alterations, but completely obliterated Jeckyll's décor by covering the priceless leather with his* Harmony in Blue and Gold, *as he called it.*

3

4

6

**(4)** *A late 19th-century interior painted by Maud Hall Neale. French- and English-style furniture co-exist with a Middle Eastern rug and an ivory inlaid Indian table with a "Benares" brass tray top. The fireplace has an Arts and Crafts mahogany surround and gilt Regency overmantel.*

**(5)** *An attic bedroom at Kelmscott Manor, the country retreat rented by William Morris and D.G. Rossetti from 1871. The green-stained furniture was designed by Ford Madox Brown and the curtain fabric is by Morris & Co.; the patchwork bed cover is American.*

**(6)** *Scarisbrick Hall, Lancashire (1837-45), was A.W.N. Pugin's thoroughgoing attempt to re-create a medieval manor house, accurate down to the last painted chevron and complete with minstrels' gallery, screens passage and louvre in the roof of the great hall.*

# DECORATIVE OBJECTS

## PAPIER MÂCHE

A hard material made from compressed and baked paper pulp had been known in Europe since the 17th century, and in 1772 Henry Clay of Birmingham patented an improved method of producing papier mâché panels which could be japanned and painted. He subsequently produced a large number of trays of all shapes and sizes.

The firm of Jennens & Bettridge took over Clay's factory in 1816 and during the 1830s and 1840s they further developed the technical and decorative possibilities of papier mâché, registering patents for many

new techniques, including inlaying. The brightly coloured naturalistic painting of flowers on this lustrous black music Canterbury of c. 1860 is enhanced by inlays of mother-of-pearl and gilded decoration.

Many other firms, mostly based in Birmingham or Wolverhampton, produced similarly decorative papier mâché wares ranging from trays and boxes to chairs, tables and other furniture. They were decorated in colours and gilding in a great variety of styles, and often by well-known painters.

2

*(1)* African Elephant *(c. 1855)* *by Antoine-Louis Barye, the leading* animalier *sculptor of the time. These lively and naturalistic animal subjects, cast as small bronzes, were immensely popular on both sides of the Channel.* *(2)* *A pair of bronze chimney ornaments in the Renaissance tradition designed by Alfred Stevens, and made by Hoole & Co., the Sheffield ironfounders and manufacturers of stoves, grates and fenders. From 1850-57 Stevens was the firm's chief designer, gaining for their products an international reputation for "good taste".*

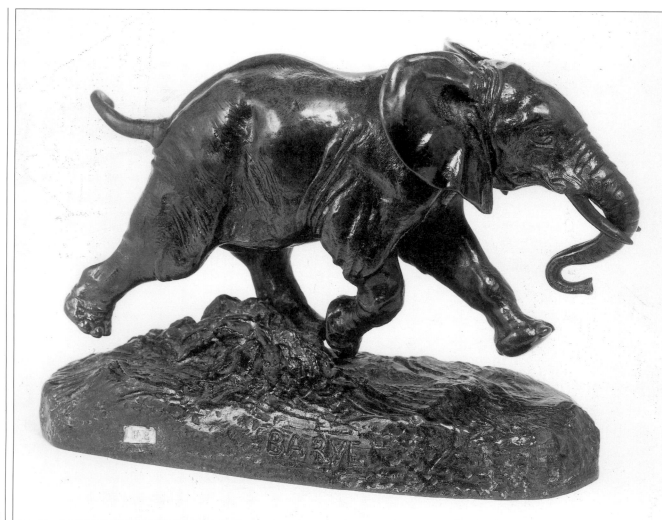

1

**(3)** *A tea chest decorated with patterns of flowers and leaves in penwork, a technique which began in the late 18th century as a way of imitating Indian ivory inlaid decoration, and soon became a favourite amateur pastime. The habit of covering boxes, small cabinets and furniture such as chess tables with elaborate penwork designs, usually in black and white, but sometimes in colours, continued for most of the Victorian period.*

3

4

5

**(5)** *A Tunbridge-ware rosewood box inlaid with a parquetry design surrounded by mosaic borders of flowers, c. 1850. The town of Tunbridge in Kent had been known for its souvenir woodware since the 17th century, and the mosaic ware produced from the 1820s onwards maintained its popularity throughout the 19th. These mosaics, reminiscent of Berlin woolwork, were made by forming designs — topographical views, butterflies, birds and animals as well as flowers — from variously coloured sticks of wood glued together and then cut transversely to form a panel. This was then glued, like a veneer, to the surface of the box or other object to be decorated.*

**(4)** *A bronze group by the Italian sculptor Antonion Giovanni Lanzirotti, c. 1870. Sentimental subjects like this naked little girl teaching her dog to beg were much favoured for domestic decoration.*

# THE VICTORIAN BATHROOM

**(1)** *A cast-iron bath with "superior coloured decorations", and a Baroque-footed bath **(2)** illustrated in the catalogue of Shanks & Co for 1899. The catalogue states that "the decorations may be applied to any of our roll-edge cast-iron baths."*

**(3)** *A "luxurious, attractive" bathroom from the Shanks' catalogue, where it is described as "Decorated Porcelain Bath, with nickel-plated fittings, Marble Lavatory Stand, Porcelain Bidet, Closet and Cistern, complete."*

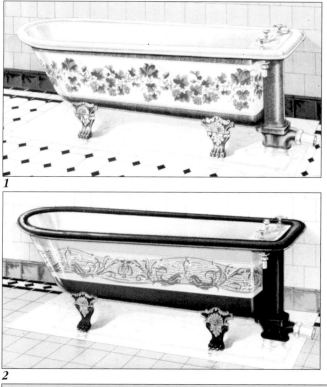

1

3

2

**(4)** *Two of Shanks's "Improved Hospital Baths ... The wheels are fitted with rubber tyres so that the Bath may be taken to the bedside of the patient." Prices ranged from £5 to £14; decoration was 10s. extra.*

4

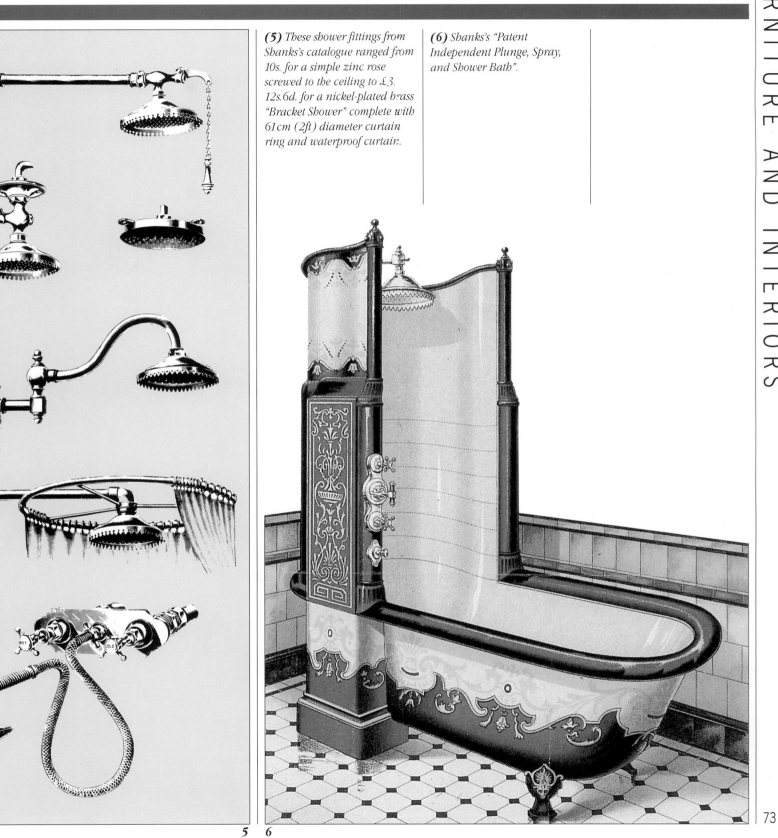

**(5)** *These shower fittings from Shanks's catalogue ranged from 10s. for a simple zinc rose screwed to the ceiling to £3. 12s.6d. for a nickel-plated brass "Bracket Shower" complete with 61cm (2ft) diameter curtain ring and waterproof curtain.*

**(6)** *Shanks's "Patent Independent Plunge, Spray, and Shower Bath".*

# ARTS AND CRAFTS

*(1)* An oak cabinet on stand by C.F.A. Voysey, late 19th century. This is a good example of the restraint and simplicity of much Arts and Crafts furniture in contrast to the ponderously fussy styles of the high Victorian period: straight lines and "revealed" construction tended to take the place of elaborate carving and veneers.

*(2)* A cabinet of rosewood inlaid with purplewood, tulipwood and ebony, designed by W.A.S. Benson and made by Morris & Co. c.1899. Primarily a designer and manufacturer of metalwork, Benson became chairman of Morris & Co. after William Morris's death in 1896, and he then designed furniture and wallpapers for the firm.

2

**3**

## MORRIS AND CO.

In 1859 William Morris married and, with the help of his friend the architect Philip Webb, built and furnished The Red House, Bexleyheath. Out of this project grew his firm, Marshall, Morris, Faulkner & Company, whose furniture, fabrics, wallpapers, metalwork, stained glass and other domestic and church furnishings became a beacon for progressive design and the embodiment of the Arts and Crafts philosophy.

The firm's early furniture designers included Ford Madox Brown, Holman Hunt and Philip Webb, while Rossetti and Burne-Jones often provided painted decoration. Later Morris devoted his personal energies to the design of wallpapers, textiles and printed books — and to socialism — but his firm, re-organized as Morris & Co. in 1875, continued to produce furniture of high quality if not always of obvious Arts and Crafts ideology.

One of the firm's chief designers of furniture towards the end of the 19th century was George Jack, whose escritoire is illustrated here. It is decorated in marquetry of sycamore and other woods, with a swirling pattern of leaves and branches strongly reminiscent of Morris's designs.

*(3) Mahogany dining chair designed by A.H. Mackmurdo for the Century Guild and made by Collinson & Lock in 1882. In the undulating plant forms of Mackmurdo's designs — for books, furniture, wallpapers and metalwork — can be seen the first stirrings of Art Nouveau. (4) An oak gateleg table by Sidney Barnsley, exhibited at the Arts and Crafts Exhibition in 1896. The furniture-making partnership of Sidney and Earnest Barnsley and Ernest Gimson continued the Arts and Crafts tradition into the 20th century.*

**4**

**5**

*(5) An oak wardrobe in the revived Queen Anne style by Gilbert Ogilvie for the Guild of Handicraft, the co-operative group of artist-craftsmen founded by C.R. Ashbee in 1888.*

# ART NOUVEAU

1

2

3

*(1)* Liberty's "Sigebert" table
(1899), of oak with fret-cut
tulip motifs on the three legs. It
was probably designed by
Leonard Wyburd, who directed
Liberty's furnishing and
decorating studio from 1883.
The firm was at the forefront of
progressive design, first in the
Japanese taste and later in the
development of Art Nouveau —
which was actually known as
Stile Liberty in Italy.

*(2)* The attenuated lines of
these ebonized and caned
chairs of c. 1896 show the
influence of the Glasgow School
of Art, where their designer
George Walton trained. He
became a close collaborator of
Mackintosh, and his furniture
was sold both by Liberty and
through his own firm of
"Ecclesiastical and House
Decorators". *(3)* Domino table
and barrel-shaped chairs
(1897) by Charles Rennie
Mackintosh, architect and
designer, who was a pivotal
figure in the development of Art
Nouveau in Europe.

**(5)** A chair of the flowing organic style associated with Continental Art Nouveau. It was designed, c. 1900 by Eugène Gaillard, a French decorator and associate of Samuel Bing.

5

**(6)** An oak cabinet with decorative panels of repoussé, brass and stained glass, by Charles Rennie Mackintosh, 1898. The stylized roses were favourite motifs, while the characteristically narrow doors give elegant proportions to a basically horizontal shape.

4

**(4)** An ash screen with carved and marquetry decoration by Emile Gallé. Like Christopher Dresser, Gallé was a botanist, and plant forms featured strongly in his work. He was most celebrated for glass and pottery, but he set up a furniture workshop in 1884 in Nancy, for which some marquetry designs were supplied by his friend Victor Prouvé.

6

# WALLPAPER

**(1)** Rowan, *a hand-screen-printed reproduction of a wallpaper by C.F.A. Voysey, 1901, originally by Charles Knowles & Co.*

*Sandersons, who took over the wallpaper manufacturing firms of William Woollams, Jeffrey & Co. and Charles Knowles, retain the archives of all three, which* contain the designs of many of the leading artists of the 19th century, including William Morris.

1

*This Japanese-inspired design of herons and swirling water* **(2)** *for a wallpaper by Arthur Silver (c. 1890) would have been considered suitable for an aesthetic dining room. Walter Crane's* Peacock Garden *wallpaper of 1899* **(3)** *was printed by Jeffrey & Co, a leading manufacturer of wallpaper whose director, Metford Warner, did much to encourage progressive design. Artists he commissioned included William Burges, E.W. Godwin, Bruce Talbert, Christopher Dresser, Walter Crane, Lewis F. Day, A.H. McMurdo and C.F.A. Voysey, and he was the printer of most of Morris's wallpaper designs.*

2

3

5

6

Christopher Dresser began his career as a botanist, and plant forms appear again and again in his work. In this design for a wallpaper **(5)** they are used within a striking pattern reminiscent of Islamic motifs. Unlike most of his contemporaries, Dresser used historical and geographical influences with refreshing simplicity and without the slavish historicism typical of his times. **(6)** Time Was, a Sanderson machine-printed wallpaper based on an anonymous Victorian flowery design.

**(4)** Silver Studio design in the aesthetic taste for the decoration of a door and wall (c. 1885). The practice of dividing the interior wall into dado, filling and frieze sections, each decorated in a different colour or pattern, was recommended by Charles Locke Eastlake in Hints on Household Taste (1867). Earlier, rooms had often been painted or papered from floor to ceiling without a break.

4

79

# FURNISHING FABRICS

(2) A Silver Studio woven silk and cotton doublecloth, 1898, with a design of swirling and stylized briar roses and other plants in alternating stripes. French textile manufacturers especially favoured such patterns, and this design was sold to the firm of Leborgne in 1898. (3) A design for a printed textile, 1892, in Arthur Silver's Japanese mood.

1

(1) A woven silk and cotton cloth in the Art Nouveau style by the distinguished Silver Studio designer John Illingworth Kay, c. 1900. Besides furnishing fabrics, Kay designed wallpapers, stencils and book covers; he was a member of the Art Workers' Guild and a keen watercolourist. The Silver Studio was one of the leading British sources of Art Nouveau in the 1890s, and the designs of Kay, together with those of Harry Napper, were widely circulated on the Continent as well as in Britain.

3

4

*(4) William Morris's "African Marigold" design, 1876, a hand-block-printed cotton originally dyed by Thomas Wardle of Leek, Staffordshire. The characteristic soft colours of Morris's printed textiles were largely achieved by vegetable dyes, and through his personal enthusiasm and experimental research Morris eventually mastered this ancient technology. (6) A design for a Liberty fabric and wallpaper by Archibald Knox, 1897. Although he is principally associated with metalwork designs in the Celtic style, notably in Liberty's Cymric silver and Tudric pewter ranges, Knox also designed carpets, textiles and jewellery.*

*(5) This simple Voysey-inspired pattern of stylized peacocks and trees on a light ground was probably by Harry Silver, son of Arthur who, with his brother Rex, ran the Silver Studio from 1901-16.*

5

6

1

**(1)** *Mahogany firescreen and pole screen carved in the mid-19th-century Rococo style and panelled with Berlin woolwork embroidery. Berlin woolwork required no artistic talent and no more than basic needlecraft to accomplish its tent- or cross-stitched exuberance, and ladies all over Europe and America took it up, liberally covering stools, chairs and cushions, or working bell-pulls, firescreen panels, bags, slippers and numerous small keepsakes.*

**(2)** Flora, *a small version of one of William Morris's Merton Abbey tapestries, made in 1896 (the first version was completed in 1885). Between 1878 and about 1892 William Morris devoted much of his creative energy to the revival of high-warp tapestry, "the noblest of the weaving arts", and from 1883 many were produced at his Merton Abbey workshops, most with the central figures designed by Burne-Jones, as here.*

2

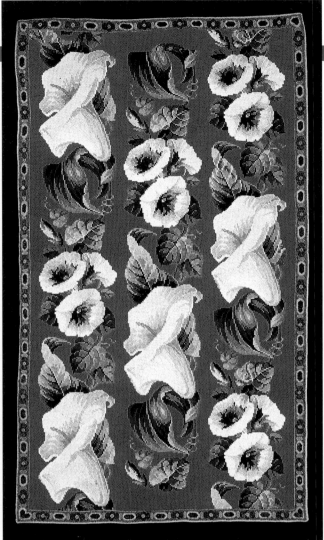

4

5

*(5) A lamp mat made in Maine, circa 1860. The central flower subject cross-stitched in Berlin woolwork is surrounded by a raised border of realistic fruits in plushwork, which involved making looped stiches and then cutting them to form a pile.*

*(4) A Berlin woolwork rug worked with a bold pattern of lilies and convolvulus against a background of the Victorians' favourite deep red, circa 1860.*

*(3) A stevengraph bookmarker of Queen Victoria framed in an elaborate combination of Gothic and "Moresque" ornament. Thomas Stevens of Coventry used a modified Jacquard loom for his woven silk pictures of royalty, politicians, historical and sporting scenes, transport and other themes which were immensely popular on both sides of the Atlantic. His factory was in production from 1854-1938.*

## LACE

Whitework and lace were both used extensively by the Victorians, for both furnishing and costume. Machine-made nets had been available since the early years of the 19th century, and were often embellished with hand embroidery. By the 1840s spotted nets and patterned laces were also being produced by machine, and many were hard to distinguish from their hand-made counterparts. In consequence, lace was more widely accessible than ever before and enjoyed huge popularity. Hand-made lace continued only in small pockets of

industry, like that of Youghal in Ireland and the established lace-making areas of Bedfordshire and Honiton. The rich continued to import lace from the Continent, and many people adapted and re-used old lace. Whitework such as Ayrshire embroidery and broderie Anglaise, much used for baby clothes, were made by hand in the early part of the period, but after the 1870s they could hardly compete with the cheap but effective machine production of Germany and Switzerland.

The illustration shows a hand-made reticella insertion in a linen tablecloth, dated 1868-81 and embroidered with the names Jack and Lola, probably commemorating a marriage or a wedding anniversary.

Flowers and Fruit, *an albumen print by Roger Fenton, described in his own lifetime as "the Turner of photography". Although better known as a topographical and war photographer, Fenton made a series of sumptuous still life photographs between 1860 and 1862, the year he gave up photography altogether and returned to his legal career.*

# CHAPTER FOUR

# PAINTING, PHOTOGRAPHY AND PRINTING

**1**

*(1)* The Deluge *by William Etty. While large-scale classical scenes were regarded as acceptable vehicles of nudity, some of Etty's naked females scandalized the Victorian public.*

But within the artistic intelligentsia questions were being raised about the usefulness of art for moral and educational purposes and about the effects of machinery on the applied arts, by artists and critics alike. Like Dickens, many were deeply disturbed by the social abuses of the age. Paintings like Richard Redgrave's *The Poor Teacher* (1843) or *The Sempstress* (1844) were designed to prick the public conscience.

The Victorians sought a spiritual solution — as always — in history. Certain artists, like the Gothic architects of the period, looked to medievalism for a message, echoing the Nazarenes, a group of German painters who, in the early years of the 19th century, had gone to Rome and practised their art within a quasi-monastic life.

### Widening horizons

In 1848 a group of young British artists — Dante Gabriel Rossetti, John Everett Millais and William Holman Hunt — found themselves in revolt against the technical laziness and triviality of contemporary fashionable art, and (like the Nazarenes 40 years earlier) very much in sympathy with Italian art of the 15th century.

They resolved on a revival of the spiritual and poetic qualities of these primitives, scorning academic rules in favour of "childlike submission to nature". With William Michael Rossetti, Thomas Woolner, James Collinson and Frederick George Stephens, they formed the Pre-Raphaelite Brotherhood. Their early disciples included Ford Madox Brown, Arthur Hughes, Walter Deverell, Frederick Sandys and Charles Collins, and by the end of the 1850s William Morris and Edward Burne-Jones were also part of the group.

Their medievalism was laughed at, their untraditional scriptural scenes were regarded as irreverent and their colours crude. Yet as early as 1849 and 1850, Pre-Raphaelite paintings were hung in the Royal Academy. By 1853 they had secured the critical approval of Ruskin, and their respectability was assured. Pre-Raphaelite influence even helped to set genre painting on a new course of moralizing and social realism, seen best in the paintings of George Elgar Hicks, Hubert von Herkomer, Luke Fildes and Frank Holl.

Greater opportunities for travel made art more exotic in subject and more open to cosmopolitan influences. Classical subjects with their legitimate nudity were also popular. Frederick Leighton was the first in a celebrated line of painters which included Edward Poynter, Lawrence Alma-Tadema, Albert Moore and John William Godward. Their sensual depictions of life in ancient Greece and Rome found an eager market among the sexually repressed Victorians.

The influence of Japan — no longer a closed country after the 1850s — was crucial not just in affecting late Victorian domestic design through the Arts and Crafts and

Nature as a source of artistic inspiration was virtually an English discovery. Lawrence, Bonington and Constable made a profound impact abroad, particularly on the succeeding generation of French painters. (Turner was a figure apart, and the poetic Samuel Palmer was another lone voice.) English painting between about 1830 and 1860 consisted chiefly of three types: idealized landscape, sentimental anecdote or realistic scenes from everyday life.

Painters like David Wilkie, Thomas Webster, Daniel Maclise, Edwin Landseer, William Mulready, Augustus Egg, John Linnell and William Powell Frith supplied the market with paintings that were easily comprehensible, well crafted in every detail, sometimes humorous, sometimes nostalgic, and wildly popular. On the classical side Benjamin Robert Haydon was a largely unsuccessful campaigner for "sublime" history painting, while William Etty favoured mythological subjects with their opportunities for painting female nudes.

**2**

"aesthetic" movements, but on the whole international course of painting. A seminal figure in this was the American-born but Paris-trained James Abbot McNeill Whistler, who brought the Impressionist influence of Monet and Degas to England.

The work of the English Impressionists in the late 19th century could be seen as a continuation of both the English traditions of landscape painting and genre, but it was much more cosmopolitan than that. Many English artists studied abroad and were imbued with the *plein-air* methods of the Barbizon School and the Impressionists, or the social realist principles of the Hague School. Walter Sickert and Philip Wilson Steer were among several English painters who were closely associated with individual French artists — Sickert with Degas and Steer with Monet.

### Photography

It was largely coincidental that the two photographic processes, the daguerreotype in France and the calotype in England, were patented in the same year (1839), for they were very different. Daguerre's method produced a one-off image on silvered copper, while Fox-Talbot's gave a negative image on coarse-grained paper which could be reproduced many times. Interestingly, the term

"photogenic drawing" was used to describe these early photographs and it was as a new means of recording existing artistic ideas that photography was at first seen.

While many of the early photographers tended to fit their images into the current painting moulds of genre, history or sentimental narrative, the best examples — by David Octavius Hill and Robert Adamson, Thomas Keith, Roger Fenton and William Grundy among others — were rarely as self-conscious as the "art" photography of the 1850s and 1860s.

While "artistic" photographers like Julia Margaret Cameron, Clementina Hawarden, Lewis Carroll, Henry Peach Robinson and William Lake Price continued to arrange their sitters in carefully contrived poses or to place them in "historical" settings, commercial photographers all over Europe were busy recording the faces of the general public. Their *cartes de visite* were extremely popular, rapidly eclipsing silhouettes as cheap portraiture. In the later 1860s, larger "cabinet" pictures were produced, but without quite superseding *cartes*. The opening of an immense number of commercial studios made photographs available to a much wider public. People collected stereoscopic photographs as well as *cartes de visite* or cabinet pictures of friends, families and heroes, to be placed in brass-clasped albums. Favourite images would be displayed in elaborate union or embossed leather cases, or worn in specially designed jewellery.

*(2) John Everett Millais's* The Blind Girl *is among the most poignant of Pre-Raphaelite images. Later, Millais was to turn towards more comfortably popular subjects — which earned him a fortune. (3)* Prince George's Favourites *by Sir Edwin Landseer, whose immaculately painted sentimental animal scenes topped the Victorian charts and earned him the title: "The Shakespeare of the World of Dogs".*

**3**

## Printing and Illustration

*(1)* Annie G with Jockey, *a plate for Eadweard Muybridge's* Animal Locomotion *(1887). Muybridge's work in recording moving men and animals was crucial to the development of cinematography in the 1890s, and painters of equestrian subjects were also deeply indebted to him.*

Steam-powered printing presses had been hailed as "an invention only second to that of Gutenberg himself" when introduced in the early 19th century. By its end, Linotype machines made almost as much impact on the speed of typesetting. Cheaper (and less durable) paper was produced from wood pulp instead of rags. Machines came in for bookbinding, and during the 1860s and 1870s techniques for printing on tin led to a packaging revolution.

Wood engraving, in the tradition of Thomas Bewick, was by far the most widely used method for much of the 19th century, and British craftsmanship in this sphere was influential in France as well as America. Printing in colours, from a separate wood block for each colour, had been possible for a long time before George Baxter patented his method of oil colour printing from wood blocks in 1836; his bright and glossy topographical views, portraits of royalty or genre subjects were tremendously popular. Baxter's process was used by others under

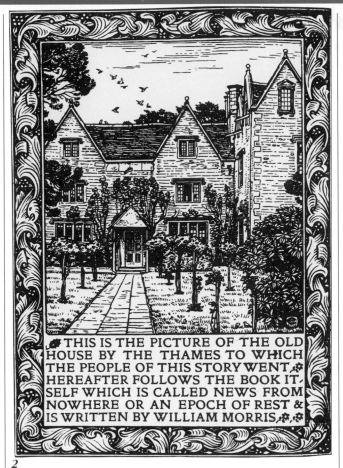

2

phy were exploited only in rare instances by the better artists in the mid-19th century; the method was in the main used by jobbing printers and mass-producers of cheap images, like the firm of Kronheim, for prints of a trivial but popular nature. An exception was Owen Jones' lavish *Grammar of Ornament* of 1856 which contained no less than 100 large chromolithographed plates.

Steel engraving was the process usually employed for reproducing the works of contemporary artists, many of whom sold the reproduction copyrights of their pictures to publishers like Colnaghi or the Belgian-born Gambart, a powerful figure in the Victorian art world. He paid the huge sum of £5,500 for Holman Hunt's *Christ Found in the Temple* (1860) — then the highest price ever paid for a modern painting — and proceeded to print it 14,000 times.

*(2) The title page of William Morris's Utopian glimpse,* News from Nowhere *(1891), one of the first books published by his influential Kelmscott Press. (3) A hand-coloured lithograph of convolvulus and ipomea from* The Ladies' Flower-Garden *(1842), one of a number of botanical and gardening manuals by Jane Loudon, wife of J.C. Loudon.*

licence, and after his death by Abraham Le Blond, who bought a number of his plates, but did not deliver the same quality. The wood block method was used pre-eminently for children's book illustration in the 1870s and 1880s. In this field the names of artists like Walter Crane, Kate Greenaway and Randolph Caldecott are legendary, and their work, often in colour, has been reproduced almost continuously ever since.

### Lithography

Lithography, invented by Aloys Senefelder of Munich in 1798, had been popularized for decorative prints by Rudolph Ackermann and Charles Hullmandel among others subsequently, and by the 1830s was being used most effectively for topographical prints and illustrations for travel books. J.D. Harding, Louis Haghe and John Frederick Lewis were among the most successful exponents of the type, while Thomas Shotter Boys was one of the first to make use of colour lithography in his *Picturesque Architecture in Paris, Ghent, Antwerp, Rouen . . .* (1839).

More often, black-and-white lithographs were hand-coloured. The decorative possibilities of chromolithogra-

3

# NARRATIVE

1

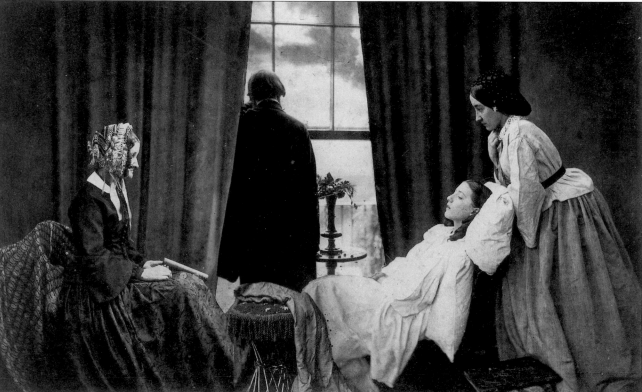

**(1)** A Summer Day in Hyde Park *(1858) by John Ritchie, a painter mainly pre-occupied with historical genre scenes set in the 16th or 17th century. In this dazzling evocation of London life in the 1850s he showed his mastery of finely observed social detail as well as a Pre-Raphaelite intensity of colour.*

**(2)** Fading Away, *an albumen print of 1858 by Henry Peach Robinson, a "high art" photographer who produced sentimental scenes to rival any painter. They were unfailingly popular, and later, Sir Luke Fildes's painting of a similar subject,* The Doctor, *was acknowledged to be "the painting of the year" when it was shown at the 1891 Royal Academy.*

2

**3**

**(3)** A Lover and his Lass *by Walter Langley, whose late 19th-century views of life in and around Newlyn in Cornwall are imbued with his warmth of feeling for the poor and hardworking people that he found there. He was one of the founders of the Newlyn School, whose main influence came from the French and from Dutch realist traditions.*

**(4)** *"Hunt the Slipper at Neighbour Flamborough's" — a scene from* The Vicar of Wakefield, *recreated by Daniel Maclise, Victorian historical and literary painter. He usually favoured the medieval or Jacobean periods, but here he gives a Victorian glimpse of the 18th century: Goldsmith's play was published in 1761.*

**(5)** He is Gone — *a hand-coloured stereo card of the 1860s. Scenes such as this, viewed through a stereoscope, appeared in three dimensions. During the 1850s and 60s stereoscopic photography was immensely popular and led to all kinds of carefully posed compositions — including the obscene. Travel views, still lifes, portraits and genre subjects were the most usual.*

**5**

**4**

# WAR AND PEACE

**2**

**1**

**(1)** The 82nd Battery Crossing Modder River, 1900, *a photograph by Captain J.A. Holson taken during the Boer War. By this time, the availability of celluloid roll film meant that spontaneous scenes of action could be photographed. William Russell's vivid reports in* The Times *about the appalling conditions of British soldiers in the Crimea prompted the British Government to send Roger Fenton **(2)** on a photographic expedition in the hope that his views might put a rosier complexion on the situation. However, many of Fenton's images showed conditions with a new realism. No restrictions were placed on the American photographer Matthew Brady **(3)**, who was able to record the tragedy of the American Civil War with even greater truth.*

**3**

**4**

**5**

**6**

(4) Gathering Waterlilies, *a platinum print made in 1887 by the East Anglian photographer Peter Henry Emerson, whose idealized images of rural life evoked a world that was fast disappearing.* (5) Sellers of Fruit and Flowers on the Cloister Lawn, Lacock, c. *1845, a calotype by William Henry Fox Talbot, whose discovery of the negative-positive process is still the basis of photography today. Unlike the daguerreotype, a one-off process, the calotype allowed multiple prints to be made from a single negative, but exposure times of several minutes made the skills of Fox Talbot and his contemporaries the more remarkable.*

(6) *A beach scene by the French-born wood engraver Paul Martin, whose unpretentious snapshots of late Victorian life brought a new* "actuality" *into photography. His work was possible through developments in the dry-plate process and the emergence of the hand camera.*

# SOCIAL CONSCIENCE

**(1)** *"Bluegate Fields", one of Gustave Doré's illustrations for* London, a Pilgrimage *(1872). Blanchard Jerrold, who wrote the text, described how "We spent many days and nights visiting and carefully examining the most striking scenes and phases of London life ..."*

**(2)** Applicants for Admission to a Casual Ward *by Sir Luke Fildes. The artist had made his living as a black-and-white illustrator for magazines until this painting was shown in the Royal Academy in 1874. It established Fildes's reputation as one of the new social realist painters.*

1

2

**(3)** The Underground Railway *by the American painter Charles G. Webber. The picture and its title describe the system by which escaped slaves from the southern states were* conveyed northwards across America through chains of "safe" houses, to Canada and freedom. The slave trade persisted in the south until the end of the American Civil War.

3

*(4) Ellen Carr aged 11, photographed on admission to one of Dr Barnardo's Homes in 1893. The philanthropist commissioned before and after photographs of all the children taken into his care from 1870 onwards: they were used not merely for records in each child's history, but also for publicizing the work of the homes.*

4

*(5)* The Sempstress *by Richard Redgrave, 1846, an interpretation of Hood's poem,* "The Song of the Shirt", *and one among several sincere attempts by the artist "at calling attention to the trials and struggles of the poor and the oppressed". When the original version of* The Sempstress *was shown at the Royal Academy in 1844 its message impressed both public and critics, just as Hood's poem had on its first publication in the Christmas 1843 number of* Punch.

5

# PORTRAIT PHOTOGRAPHY

1

2

*(1) A cowboy trail boss in Montana, about 1888. As the century progressed photographers benefited from shorter exposure times to produce pictures of greater spontaneity. (2) Alexander Hester's portrait of Abraham Lincoln, then presidential nominee, June 1860, Springfield, Illinois, and (3) the President's wife, Mary Todd Lincoln, photographed in her inaugural gown by Matthew Brady, 1861.*

3

## DAGUERREOTYPES

Although Fox-Talbot's discovery of the negative-positive process of photography had a much greater influence on subsequent developments, Daguerre's method, announced in 1839, was at first the more popular. Each image was unique and could not be reproduced like the calotype, but the result was superior in clarity of detail. During the 1840s portrait studios were opened by daguerreotypists all over Europe and in America, and the well-to-do flocked to sit for their likenesses. These were presented behind glass in plush-lined cases of leather, papier-mâché, mother-of-pearl or other material to protect the delicate silvered surface of the pictures.

Among the most fashionable daguerreotype portrait studios in London were those of Richard Beard, Antoine Claudet, John Jabez Edwin Myall and William Edward Kilburn, the last notable for delicate hand-tinted images. Claudet, whose portrait of his partner's grandmother, c. 1850, is shown here, became "Photographer-in-ordinary to the Queen" in 1853.

By the late 1850s the daguerreotype had had its day, overtaken by the wet-plate process introduced in 1851, which combined the clarity of the daguerreotype with the possibilities of reproduction of the calotype.

*(4) An albumen print of the actress Ellen Terry (1868) by Julia Margaret Cameron, one of the great early portrait photographers, whose soft-focus images of well-known Victorians are celebrated. Her aim was "to ennoble photography and to secure for it the character and uses of High Art by combining the real and the ideal and sacrificing nothing of Truth by all possible devotion to Poetry and Beauty." This work is in striking contrast to* Gettysburg Hero *(5), a stark, unglamorized portrait of John L. Burns by O'Sullivan, 1863.*

4

5

6

7

*(6) Lady Henry Somerset (1858-59), an albumen print by Lewis Carroll, as celebrated for his sensitive portraits as he is for* Alice in Wonderland. *He was a friend of Julia Margaret Cameron, and like her, he photographed many of his famous contemporaries, but his favourite sitters were little girls, the best known of whom was Alice Liddell. (7) John MacCosh, a surgeon on the Bengal Establishment, was probably the first British war photographer. He took up photography while stationed in the Himalayas in 1844, and during the Second Sikh War (1848-49) he produced a number of small portraits, later progressing to topographical views.*

# PRESENTATION

**(1)** *An olive-wood fan decorated with fretwork for displaying cartes de visite. Collecting cartes became a national craze during the 1860s; many were kept in decorative albums, but single and multiple frames were also produced for displaying them.*

**(2)** *A portrait daguerreotype by Gustave Nehme, a pupil of Daguerre, displayed in a relief-moulded and gilt frame in the Rococo style of the 1840s.*

**(3)** *Two ambrotypes of the Paten family displayed in gilt frames in a paired leather case of the 1850s. After 1851 photographers benefited from the introduction of Frederick Scott Archer's collodion or wet-plate process which, using a glass negative, combined the clarity of the daguerreotype with the facility for reproduction of the calotype; the resulting positives were known as ambrotypes.*

1

2

3

*(4) A folding leather frame for four cartes de visite, c. 1875.*

**5**

*(5) An 1850s daguerreotype portrait of an American lady by Richards of Philadelphia, in a shaped gilt frame protected by a plush-lined leather case. (6) Treasure Spots of the World, 1875, a collection of 28 photographs assembled by Walter Bentley Woodbury and illustrated by his Woodburytype process.*

**6**

# HISTORICAL THEMES

**(1)** A Picture Gallery *by Sir Lawrence Alma-Tadema, the prolific Dutch-born painter of Greek and Roman scenes that were immensely popular with late 19th-century audiences on both sides of the Atlantic. Of great technical brilliance, their* painstaking archaeological and architectural accuracy was made possible by such publications as *The Ruins and Excavations of Ancient Rome: A Companion Book for Students and Travellers (1897) by Rodolfo Lanciani.*

**(2)** King Cophetua and the Beggar Maid *by Daniel Maclise, 1869. Maclise was the archetypal Victorian history painter, whose vivid recreations of historical, literary and romantic legend appealed to the period's taste for nostalgia.*

4

5

(3) Mary Queen of Scots attended by Rizzio, *a photograph by Victor Albert Prout. The two "models" are the Hon. Lewis Wingfield and Miss G. Moncrieffe, posing to entertain the Prince and Princess of Wales in 1863.*
(4) Don Quixote in His Study, 1857, by the "high art" photographer William Lake Price, who specialized in elaborately contrived historical evocations. (5) Mercy: David Spareth Saul's Life *(1854) by Richard Dadd, whose mental illness confined him first to Bethlem and later to Broadmoor for 43 years.*

# THE TRAVELLERS

(1) *Edward Lear's watercolour view of Scindia Ghat, Benares, dated 1875. Lear's extensive travels took him to many parts of southern Europe and to the Middle East, and between 1873 and 1875 he travelled in India and Ceylon, invited there by the* viceroy, Lord Northbrook. (2) *"The Colossus at Java" — a Woodburytype illustration from* Treasure Spots *by Walter Bentley Woodbury, who lived in Australia and later in Java. He was the inventor of a mechanical method of* reproducing photographs which was used for illustrating many publication in the 1870s.

1

2

(3) Sculptures at Dendera, Egypt, *1857, an albumen print by Francis Frith, one of the great travelling photographers of the 19th century. He made extensive journeys in the Middle East and later his views of towns and villages all over Britain were on sale in over 2,000 shops.*

3

*(4) "Ice Cavern", a Woodburytype illustration from a negative by the Alpine photographer Adolphe Braun in Treasure Spots, 1875.*

4

5

*(5)* A Hilly Landscape in Palestine, *1846, a painting by Hubert Settler. Undeterred by privation and discomfort, large numbers of artists and photographers were lured to the Middle East by its exotic landscapes, momentous archaeology and colourful people. (6)* The Hareem *by John Frederick Lewis, one of the most accomplished watercolourists of the 19th century, who travelled in Spain, Greece and the Middle East before settling in Cairo in 1841. He lived there in the guise of a Turk for nearly 10 years and left an unparalled legacy of watercolour scenes of Egyptian life.*

6

# THE PRE-RAPHAELITES

**(1)** Bower Meadow *by Dante Gabriel Rossetti who, with William Holman Hunt and John Everett Millais, was a founding member of the Pre-Raphaelite Brotherhood. The sensuous-lipped and Titian-haired women in his allegorical paintings were often portrayals of the women in his life, particularly William Morris's wife, Jane, and his own wife, Elizabeth Siddall. Although he considered himself to be primarily a poet, his influence on the painters of his own and the next generation was potent.*

1

**(2)** Burne-Jones's Earth Mother, 1882. *Edward Burne-Jones was a pupil of Rossetti, whose influence can be seen here, as well as a close associate of William Morris, for whom he painted furniture and designed stained glass and textiles. The treatment of the trees in the background of this painting is strongly reminiscent of tapestry, and at the same time presages Art Nouveau.*

2

**(3)** Christ in the House of his Parents *by John Everett Millais, 1850. Among the earliest Pre-Raphaelite paintings to be* shown at the Royal Academy, *this unconventionally poignant treatment of the Holy Family provoked a storm of hostility,* not least from Charles Dickens. *Millais later forsook Pre-Raphaelite ideals for more popular subject matter.*

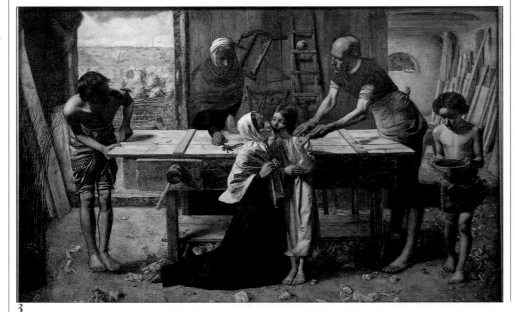

3

4

5

*(4) A sketch by William Holman Hunt for his large picture,* The Lady of Shalott, *illustrating a verse of Tennyson's poem. According to Holman Hunt, the painting's rich symbolism "illustrates the failure of a human Soul towards its accepted responsibility". Hunt's Pre-Raphaelite approach to scriptural subjects took him to the Middle East in 1854. "My desire is very strong to make more tangible Jesus Christ's history and teaching," he said, and one of the results was* The Scapegoat *(5), an illustration of the passage in Isaiah: "Surely he hath borne our Griefs and carried our Sorrows..." Hunt spent many weeks making sketches for the painting at Oosdom, on the salt-encrusted edge of the Dead Sea, with the mountains of Edom in the background.*

# ILLUSTRATION

(1) *Alphonse Mucha's sensuous cover for the Christmas 1896 edition of* L'Illustration. *This is one of the many designs he made – for magazine and book covers, posters and all kinds of publicity material – in* the distinctive style that has come to be regarded as the epitome of Art Nouveau. (2) *Cover design for the Chicago-based magazine* The Echo, *February 1896, by John Sloan.*

(3) *"Tiger Lily" from* Through the Looking Glass. *The* Punch *cartoonist Sir John Tenniel's illustrations for Lewis Carroll's "Alice" books are widely regarded as among the supreme examples of Victorian book illustration.*

1

2

3

**(4)** *"Tom Tom the Piper's Son" from Kate Greenaway's* Mother Goose. *Her instantly recognizable illustrations of a make-believe world peopled by demure and aesthetically clad innocents continue to charm modern audiences as much as they did her own.*

**(5)** *Walter Crane's figure of Hibernia, symbolizing a united Ireland, for a calendar of 1897 printed by Marcus Ward & Co for the Royal Ulster Works, Belfast.*

Tom, Tom, the piper's son,
He learnt to play when he was young,
He with his pipe made such a noise,
That he pleased all the girls and boys.

4

5

# ADVERTISING

(1) An advertisement for Viyella, c. 1900. Advances in colour printing techniques towards the end of the 19th century gave an impetus to both advertising and packaging.

(2) The American tobacco advertisement of 1867 uses the theme of reconciliation in the Civil War to convey its message.

(3) One of Jules Cheret's lithographic posters advertising the Folies Bergère, 1893. Cheret was at the forefront of the revival of the colour lithograph as a means of serious artistic expression in the 1890s. Because of chromolithography's long association with the cheap prints known as oleolithographs, self-respecting artists had to overcome a good deal of prejudice in order to exploit the process's undoubted potential.

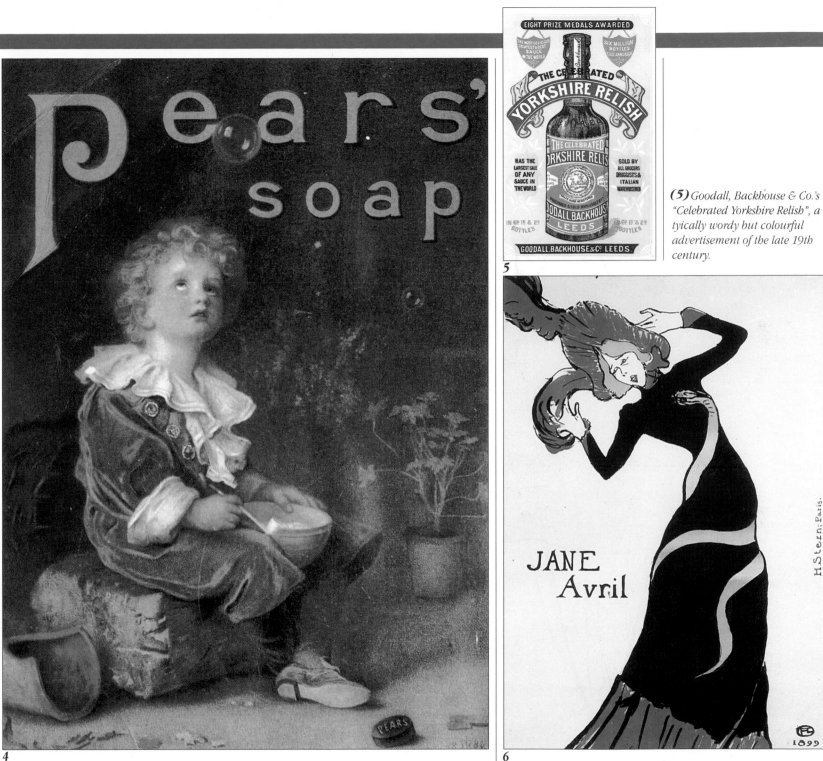

**(5)** *Goodall, Backhouse & Co.'s "Celebrated Yorkshire Relish", a tyically wordy but colourful advertisement of the late 19th century.*

**4**

**(4)** *John Everett Millais was already regarded as the most popular painter in England when he painted* Bubbles, *a portrait of his grandson, Willie James, in 1886. The previous year he had become the first artist to be created a baronet. The picture was bought by A. & F. Pears Ltd. (for £2,200) and immortalized in this famous advertisement.*

**6**

**(6)** *One of Henri de Toulouse-Lautrec's posters of the dancer Jane Avril, a life-long friend. Lautrec regarded lithography as a major art form and used it as a medium for some of his most important work. Between 1891 and 1901 he produced no less than 357 lithographs — song sheets, posters and single-sheet prints for collectors.*

# PRINTING

**1**

(1) *An engraving of William Powell Frith's painting,* The Railway Station *(1862), one of many popular works that were widely disseminated through print dealers like Gambart and Flatow. In this case L.V. Flatow commissioned the painting on the strength of Frith's preliminary oil sketch, and paid £4,500 for it. The scene includes several minor dramas, such as the criminal being arrested, and there are also portraits of Frith himself and his family (left and centre).* (2) Grosvenor Gate, Hyde Park, *a hand-coloured lithograph by Thomas Shotter Boys, one of the accomplished group of topographical artists of the 1830s and 40s whose work was reproduced by the relatively new lithographic process. His* Original Views of London As It Is *was published in 1842.*

**2**

3

*(3)* The Ascent of Mont Blanc, *an example of George Baxter's process of printing in oil colours from engraved wood blocks, patented in 1836. His bright and glossy topographical views, portraits of royalty and genre subjects were tremendously popular.*

4

*(4) The letter O from* An Alphabet *by William Nicholson, 1898. Nicholson and his brother-in-law James Pryde formed the partnership of the Beggerstaff Brothers, producing memorably bold images in black, generally on tinted backgrounds. Nicholson used a woodcut technique for his poster designs and book illustrations, and the printing was done by lithography.*

*(5) A.H. Mackmurdo's undulating design for the title-page of* Wren's City Churches *(1883) was revolutionary at the time and is regarded as the first manifestation of Art Nouveau. Mackmurdo was an active member of the Society for the Protection of Ancient Buildings which had been founded by William Morris in 1877.*

5

## ETCHING

Many artists, including some whose works were reproduced for the popular market by the steel engravers, turned to etching as a means of personal artistic expression. The influence of 17th-century Dutch painter-etchers like Rembrandt was strong, and so was the reaction against the highly commercial popular print market. The Etching Club, formed in 1836, and its offshoot the Junior Etching Club, united a disparate group of artists who produced illustrations to literary works such as Goldsmith's *The Deserted Village* (1841) and *Songs and Ballads of Shakespeare* (1843), as well as etchings for the Art Union.

The poetic landscapes of Samuel Palmer show most fully the subtle nuances of light and shade

that such a consummately skilled artist could achieve in the etching process, which even gained popularity with amateurs, including Queen Victoria, to whom Landseer imparted the technique.

The Pre-Raphaelite's journal,

*The Germ,* was illustrated with etchings. Holman Hunt and Millais were the keenest of the Brotherhood, but many of their followers, including Simeon Solomon, William Bell Scott and James Smetham in the 1850s and 1860s, were also smitten. During the same period Whistler and his brother-in-law Seymour Haden were breathing a new life and spontaneity into etching, moving away from the anecdotal tradition towards a style based on observation, in which mood and atmosphere become as important as the scene depicted. Whistler's etching shown here, *The Embroidered Curtain* (1889), demonstrates his technical virtuosity as well as his debt to 17th-century Dutch art.

# GREETINGS

1

2

(1) *A Valentine card of the 1860s, inscribed "I love thee". A posy of flowers is framed by a elaborate confection of pierced and embossed paper with gold and silver highlights and coloured paper scraps.* (2) *A shaped Valentine, with the unpresuming legend "Hope bids me trust in thee" beneath a couple seated by a lake, is decorated with a pierced and embossed mount in blue and silver, encircled by a band of pink chenille.*

*All Happiness attend thee throughout the coming Year.*

3

4

*(6) Christmas and marriage both creep into the figurative vignettes on this flower-strewn, gold-embellished birthday card. (7) A carefree message on an 1880s birthday card.*

6

*(3) A few streaks of glitter is the only seasonal concession on this 1890s Christmas card depicting a milkmaid in a meadow. (4) Walter Crane's "Christmas Stocking for you", an appropriate greeting for the aesthetic 1870s. (5) A pair of robins sing out their Christmas greetings in this lacy paper and coloured scrap card of the 1880s.*

5

7

*A photographic portrait of Miss Maude
Millett, a young belle of 1890s society,
dressed as a debutante in flower-
bedecked white muslin and silk.*

# CHAPTER FIVE
# COSTUME AND JEWELLERY

**1**

Throughout the Victorian period, France was the chief arbiter of taste in women's fashions, while England dictated the contrastingly sombre styles of men's clothes. The beginnings of the ready-to-wear industry, first established in Paris in the 1820s and 1830s, spread to other parts of Europe and North America, and further threats to the traditional dominance of the dressmaker were seen in the establishment of the style-setting Parisian couture houses.

In 1858 the Englishman Charles Frederick Worth was the first to realize the potential of presenting a "collection" of models to a rich and receptive clientele, and his example was followed before the end of the century by many others, who were to spread French fashions around the world.

The classically inspired dresses of the early 19th century, with their *décolleté* necklines, high waists and loosely flowing narrow skirts, were being replaced, by the 1830s, by the upholstered fullness that characterized the Romantic style. Waists were dropped and corseted to produce hour-glass shapes, with wide boat-shaped necklines and huge "leg-of-mutton", "beret", puff or "elephant ear" sleeves above, and gathered, often flounced, skirts flowing outwards over full petticoats below.

The crinoline was introduced in 1842 to support these increasingly voluminous garments. At first it took the form of a stiff horsehair underskirt of circular shape, and later became a whalebone or metal hooped cage. By the 1850s the greatest fullness was concentrated at the back of the skirt, and this developed into the padded bustle in the 1870s and 1880s, when narrower dimensions around the hems of dresses changed the feminine silhouette completely. The re-introduction of the 18th-century polonaise or gathered overskirt, as well as draped tunics and aprons, gave these dresses a weighty and upholstered appearance, much in accord with the furnishings of the period. The 1890s saw a return of hour-glass shapes, with full sleeves and triangular flaring skirts.

### Dress for the "aesthetes"

In the 1850s William Morris designed a simple loose gown of medieval flavour for Jane Burden, later his wife, and many of the Pre-Raphaelite women adopted similarly comfortable clothes instead of the corseted and restrict-

**2**

worn by Brunel in the famous photograph) via the shiny, jaunty toppers of the 1880s to the more informal bowlers and homburgs of the end of the century, men's headgear records the passage of time.

The clothes they wore hardly varied except in small details. Black frock-coats or tails were worn with checked, striped or light-coloured, narrow-cut trousers. It was not until the 1870s that the suit — jacket, trousers and waistcoat in the same material — made its appearance, and then only for informal occasions. Later still, tweeds were worn by country sportsmen, including the Prince of Wales, who popularized the Norfolk jacket. Touches of elegance such as velvet collars, silk lapels or coloured cravats were so low-key as to pass almost unnoticed.

ing crinolines of current fashion. These were the basis of the "aesthetic" costumes of the 1880s, which, although derided by some, appealed to a widening circle of discriminating ladies.

While their tastes were catered for at Liberty's, whose dress department opened in 1884, as well as by individual dressmakers, the vast majority of women adhered to strict etiquette. Clothes and their materials varied greatly, chiefly according to the time of day, the occasion for which they were worn, and the age of the wearer.

### Men's fashions

Men's clothes underwent relatively few changes during the period. Regency dandyism gave way to the soberest of attire for Victorian men. The influence of Beau Brummell, with his "passionate moderation" and "exquisite suitability in dress", set the tone of elegant understatement and provided a plain contrast to women's clothes. Indeed, from the mid-century on, the gradual change in men's fashions can be more easily recognized by the shape of their hats than by the cut of their clothes. From the broad-brimmed, lofty "stove-pipes" (like the one

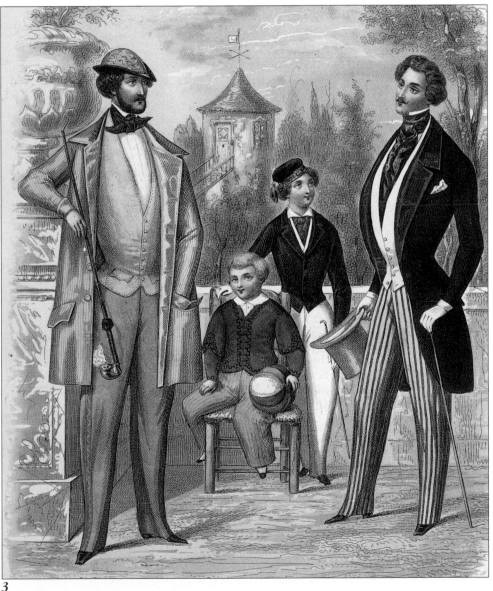

**3**

## Jewellery

Profusion and variety are the two characteristics of Victorian jewellery: never was so much worn by so many, ranging from the exotic *parures* of sparkling diamonds and precious gemstones worn by the rich to the polished pebble jewellery bought as souvenirs.

The low necklines and tight cuffs of early Victorian dresses lent themselves especially to necklaces and bracelets, but hair ornaments and earrings were also important. Later styles demanded brooches for day and evening wear, and men brightened their sombre clothes with watch-chains, fob watches and jewelled tie-pins.

Machine processes brought jewellery to the masses, while mineralogical and archaeological discoveries all over the world resulted in revivalism of technique as well as style. Pearls remained popular, as did deep red garnets. Colour was of paramount importance, and this gave a new popularity to stones such as turquoises, malachite and coral, as well as to enamelling.

Marble jewellery included Italian micro-mosaic pictures of views of Rome and other classical subjects, and colourful *pietre dure* flowers and butterflies in neatly patterned gold frames. The coloured marbles found in the Derbyshire Peak District were also used for jewellery and small objects. Carved cameos, whether in hardstones such as agate, chalcedony and sardonyx, or in shell, were favoured as a contrast to the rich, heavy fabrics of day-time dress, while materials such as jet, ivory and coral were carved with fine virtuosity.

Jet, a particularly hard form of fossilized wood found at its highest quality near Whitby in Yorkshire, was favoured most of all for mourning jewellery. It is not always easy to distinguish from bog oak, which was also carved into jewellery, or from imitations such as "French jet" (a glass-covered wax), papier mâché and ebonite, an early form of plastic made from rubber hardened with sulphur. Mourning was an important ritual for the Victorians, observed with increasing solemnity even before Prince Albert's untimely death plunged the nation into wholehearted sympathy with the Queen, and the production of mourning pieces formed a major part of the jewellers' output. Hair of the deceased was plaited, woven or coiled into gem-set mementoes and black enamel, onyx and glass were used, often in elaborate gold settings.

Decorative effects were achieved as often with settings

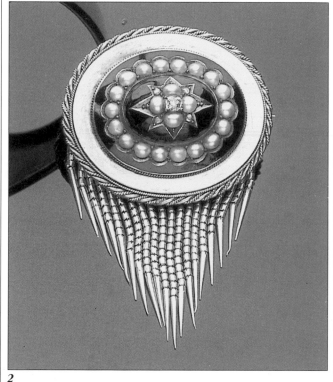

*2*

as with the gems they supported — which, after all, were not always of great intrinsic worth. There seems no end to the inventiveness and skill of the Victorian jeweller in cajoling metals into the shapes demanded by Rococo, Classical, Renaissance and Gothic styles, or the naturalistic novelties — flowers, birds, snakes, lizards, insects and even monkeys — that the Victorians loved. Cut steel, a Birmingham speciality, and the new aluminium were exploited to great effect, while the use of iron pyrites (marcasite) was developed in France.

## Archaeological jewellery

The Italian scholar-jeweller Castellani rediscovered the ancient technique of granulation, which went on to be used by a number of craftsmen in Italy and in England,

*(1)* Two brooches and a bracelet of Scottish agate, typical of the hardstone jewellery popular with the many tourists who were influenced by Queen Victoria's passion for Scotland. *(2)* A mourning brooch of pearls and diamonds set in black enamel, framed and fringed with gold, circa *1860.*

*1*

particularly for the "Etruscan" imitation jewellery fashionable in the 1860s. Castellani's compatriot, Giuliano, from Naples, worked in London during the latter half of the 19th century, producing jewellery in which reticulated gold and filigree were used with enamels, pearls and polished or carved semi-precious stones. He was at the forefront of the revival of enamelling in the Renaissance style, and his work was widely copied but rarely equalled.

The excitement of archaeological discoveries, especially Greek, Roman, Egyptian and Celtic, resulted in a spate of related jewellery in the 1850s and 1860s. That in the Assyrian taste was inspired by the publication of Sir Austen Layard's *Nineveh and its Remains* in 1849. The 16th-century jewellery designs of Hans Holbein were copied in *champlevé* enamel pendants, while in France the goldsmith Alphonse Fouquet united the skills of Limoges enameller Grandhomme and the sculptor Carrier de Belleuse in the heaviest of Renaissance-style jewels.

One of the most influential exponents of the revived art of enamelling was Alexander Fisher, who studied the old methods in France and Italy, taught in London art schools in the 1880s, and produced enamel on his own

3

account. He exhibited with the Arts and Crafts Exhibition Society in the 1890s, and his use of motifs from the fine enamelling of the ancient Celts was adopted by many Art Nouveau designers, including those of Liberty's Cymric range of silver and jewellery.

C.R. Ashbee was as important in late 19th-century jewellery as in silver design. He too exhibited with the Arts and Crafts Exhibition Society and also at the Vienna Secession, whose practical offshoot, the Wiener Werkstätte, was modelled on his Guild of Handicraft.

### Fin-de-siècle jewellery

The Art Nouveau style in jewellery is best exemplified in the work of René Lalique. He made extensive use of the difficult and fragile technique of *pliqué-à-jour* enamel-

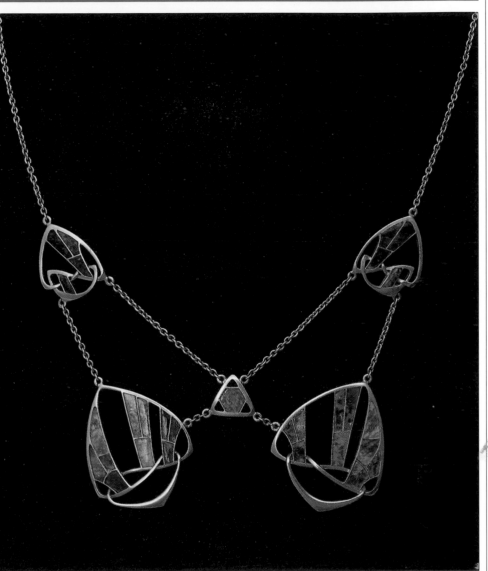

4

ling, and his plant, animal and female forms transcend mere wearable jewellery to become major works of art. Lalique's followers included Georges Fouquet (son of Alphonse), Henri Vever, Eugène Feuillâtre and Alphonse Mucha, while Tiffany of New York introduced Art Nouveau jewellery to rich and discerning American customers.

The discovery of vast diamond deposits in South Africa in the second half of the 19th century gave a fresh impetus to diamond — and imitation diamond — jewellery. Sensationally large and multi-faceted stones were set into dazzling diadems for the world's royalty, while hardly less brilliant were the tiaras and *parures* of the rich. Diamonds and their imitations were sought after by anyone and everyone.

*(3) A diamond and ruby butterfly brooch of a type especially popular towards the end of the century, and (4) a necklace of gold and opals designed by Archibald Knox for Liberty, circa 1900.*

# INSPIRATIONS

*(1) A gold and enamel brooch in the Egyptian style with a central mask. The Victorian period was one of vigorous excavation all over the Near East and southern Europe, and public interest in newly discovered artefacts resulted in a demand for "archaeological" jewellery in a number of styles.*

1

2

*(2) The entrance to the Temple, High Mound, Nineveh. Sir Henry Austen Layard's excavations in the 1850s led to* *the production of "Assyrian" jewellery. (3) Sir Edward Poynter's watercolour* Helen of Troy, *an imaginary conception* *of the famous queen, but wearing the actual gold jewellery that the archaeologist Schliemann had found in 1873.*

3

**(4)** *Gainsborough's portrait of* Mary, Countess Howe. *Fashions in women's clothes have always been revived, copied or adapted at a later date, and the draped overskirts and close-fitting bodices of the 1880s fashions are rooted in the 18th century.*

**(5)** *Hans Holbein, best known to us today as a painter, also designed silver, jewellery and stained glass. His designs, like this one for a pendant, were much imitated for the "Renaissance" jewels of the 19th century.*

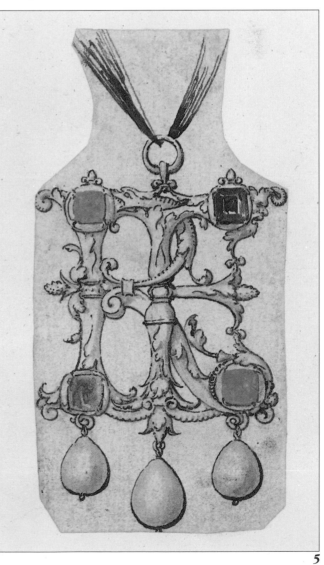

4

5

# THE LADY OF FASHION

**(1)** *A necklace of foiled pink topaz and pearls in a gold cannetille setting of the type still* *fashionable at the beginning of Queen Victoria's reign. Cannetille work was a* *progression of filigree: coils, beads and florets of gilt wire were built up to form lacy* *patterns, with or without coloured gems or pearls set into them.*

1

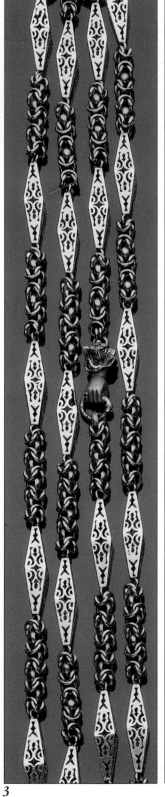

2

**(2)** *Flowers as well as jewels were worn in profusion for grand occasions. Here visitors in court dress are preparing to be received at Buckingham Palace.*

**(3)** *An early Victorian muff chain with pierced bobbin links and a gauntlet clasp set with turquoises. The hand was a symbol of friendship, frequently used in the 19th century.*

3

4

*(4) Jet jewellery and black-beaded decoration was widely used, particularly in the many periods of mourning to which the Victorians were subjected. This magazine illustration dates from about 1890.*

*(5) A bracelet of coloured golds with turquoises and rose diamonds set in an enamel-edged diaper pattern, c. 1870.*

5

*(6) A fashion plate of the early 1880s showing the upholstered look that resulted from the use of a horsehair pouf to exaggerate the bustle. Draped overskirts added to the hobbled effect.*

6

7

*(7) A diamond fly on a bright blue enamel background in a robust gold setting with gadrooned and Rococo decoration and filigree threads. This bracelet is characteristic of the eclectic style in jewellery of the 1860s and 1870s.*

123

# HIGH VICTORIAN

(1) *A plate from the* Englishwoman's Domestic Magazine *showing two smart ladies and a child in the fashions of 1868. Although their costumes are far from "aesthetic", the Japanese influence is already discernible in the vase of peacocks' feathers in the background.*

(4) *A hand-coloured* carte de visite *of the Empress of Austria. Her flounced dress, the heavy draped curtain, the Rococo flower vase and the scrolling chair-back add up to a characteristic 1860s look.*

(2) *A group of jewels in the revivalist styles of the mid-19th century.*

(3) *A mid-Victorian gold heart-shaped locket set with an emerald and rubies and surmounted by a crown set with diamonds, emeralds and rubies.*

**5**

**(5)** *A demi-parure of pavé-set diamonds and garnets in a gold setting in a Rococo-inspired design of the 1840s.*

**(6)** *A cartouche-shaped brooch with gold Rococo scrollwork and turquoises set against a matt-gold ground, c. 1840.*

**6**

**7**

**(7)** *A mid-Victorian gold bracelet made by Robert Phillips of Cockspur Street, London. Diamonds and step-cut* octagonal peridots are surrounded by red and white enamels in a distinguished interpretation of the Tudor rose motif. **(8)** *The flounced crinolines of high fashion displayed in a plate from the Magasin des Demoiselles, 1860.*

**8**

# FIN DE SIECLE

(1) A butterfly brooch set with rose diamonds and coloured stones, of a relatively inexpensive type. Small brooches such as this were often worn, several at a time, to fasten lace and other embellishments on the clothing.

1

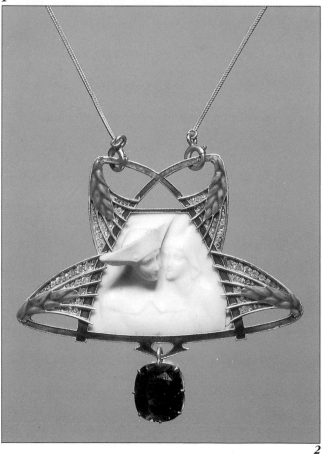

2

3

(2) In this late 19th-century pendant by René Lalique a pair of medieval figures in carved ivory are surrounded by diamond and enamel wheat ears set in gold with a single sapphire below. Lalique was pre-eminent in the distinguished hand of Art Nouveau jewellers who broke new ground in their use of materials as well as in their sensuously flowing designs and their technical virtuosity. (3) Two ladies out for a stroll, in a French fashion plate of 1889. Hats were still small, but bustles had given way to elegantly flowing skirts.

(**4**) *A silver necklace set with plaques of "lava" glass, possibly made by Tiffany, New York, c. 1900. One of the leaders in the development of Art Nouveau Tiffany's influence was felt in Europe as well as America, particularly in glassmaking.*

(**5**) *The slimmed-down silhouettes and flowing skirts of the late 1890s are apparent in these two evening gowns for young ladies from* La Mode Illustrée. (**6**) *The silver and enamel buckle in the Celtic-inspired Art Nouveau style was designed for Liberty in 1906 by Jessie M. King, a Glasgow-trained artist and friend of C.R. Mackintosh, who made designs for books, tiles, wallpaper and fabrics as well as jewellery.*

5

4

6

# COSTUME FOR SPORT

**(1)** The Amateur Bicycle Match at Lillie Bridge, *1875. Penny-farthings like these were speedy but dangerous, and bicycling only became widely popular during the 1890s after the invention of the chain-driven safety bicycle and the development of pneumatic tyres by John Dunlop.*

**(2)** *Walking for pleasure was a formal occupation and provided an opportunity for sartorial display, as is shown by this lady's walking dress from* La Mode Illustrée *(1849). Throughout the Victorian period France was the chief arbiter of taste in women's fashions.*

1

Robe avec tunique et boléro.
Modèle de M<sup>lle</sup> Louise Piret, rue Richer, 43.
(**Patrons découpés** : N° 357. Jupe. — N° 358. Corsage.)

2

**(3)** *Lawn tennis celebrities at Wimbledon 1888.and* **(4)** *Amelia Jenks Bloomer wearing her bloomer costume in a lithograph of 1851. The crinoline retained its importance for formal evening wear even after it had been* discarded in favour of more manageable clothing during the day. From its beginnings it had not been without opponents, and Amelia Bloomer, who recommended long full trousers as appropriate wear for ladies was the most colourful of these. In 1851 she displayed models of this revolutionary and emancipating attire in London and Dublin, but her ideas, too advanced for the time, were greeted with horror and derision.

3

**(5)** *Few women wore trousers except for bathing, a therapeutic occupation performed away from the prying eyes of men by means of bathing machines, which could be wheeled into the sea. The girls in this French fashion print of the 1860-70 period are the attendants.*

5

6

**(6)** *Even with their encumbering long skirts, women scurried enthusiastically about the hockey pitch in the 1890s.*

# ACCESSORIES AND HAIRSTYLES

**(1)** *"Thornhill's registered" skirt clip, a decorative way to lift flowing skirts out of the mud. This silver example is by Thomas Johnson, London, 1876.*

**(2)** *A collection of decorative telescopic pencils in a variety of styles and disguises, several were made by Sampson Mordan, who specialized in such items.*

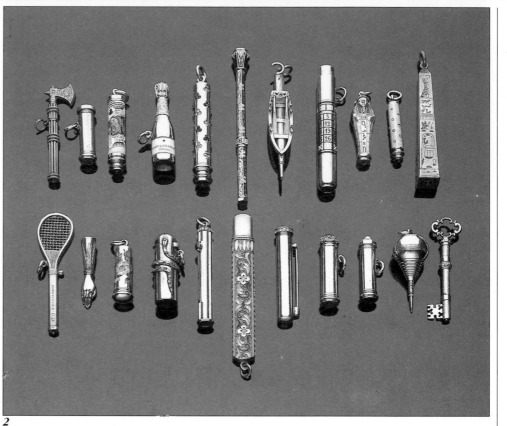

2

1

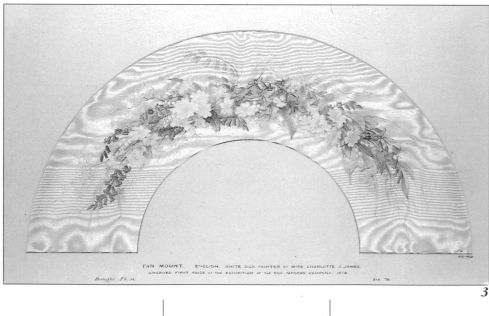

FAN MOUNT.  ENGLISH.  WHITE SILK PAINTED BY MISS CHARLOTTE J. JAMES.
AWARDED FIRST PRIZE AT THE EXHIBITION OF THE FAN MAKERS' COMPANY, 1878.

3

4

**(3)** *A white silk fan mount, delicately painted with naturalistic spring flowers by Miss Charlotte J. James. This was awarded first prize at the exhibition of the Fan Makers Company in 1878.* **(4)** *An* ostrich-feather fan, 38cm (15in.) long, offered in the catalogue of the Association of Diamond Merchants, Jewellers and Silversmiths, 1895, in a range of qualities and shades at prices from £2.2s.

**(5)** *Hats and hairstyles as well as a host of accessories gave still greater variety to the appearance of women. "Bertha" collars, fichus of lace, and Paisley or cashmere shawls were used a great deal, while* feather or fur boas gained popularity towards the end of the century. The piled-up hairstyles of the late 1890s were set off by high and often bejewelled necklines.

5

## CARD CASES

Visiting-card cases were made in great profusion throughout the Victorian period, in response to the well-established ritual of calling, with its elaborate etiquette. Personally engraved cards were kept in slim and elegant boxes made in an astonishing variety of materials and techniques. Ladies' card cases, like their cards, were customarily larger than gentlemen's.

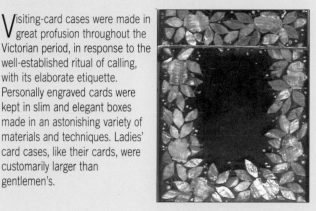

Silver, tortoiseshell, ivory, mother-of-pearl, papier mâché, wood, leather and even sealing wax were used, and practically every decorative technique known to the Victorians can be seen in these miniature masterpieces of painting, inlaying, pressing, embossing, carving or tooling. The picture shows a mid-19th-century black papier mâché case with inlaid mother-of-pearl leaves.

**(6)** *Parisian hat fashions, c. 1870, from* Le Monde Elegant. *It was not until the very end of the century that large hats became* de rigeur. *Hat fashions of the 1870-80 period* **(7)**.

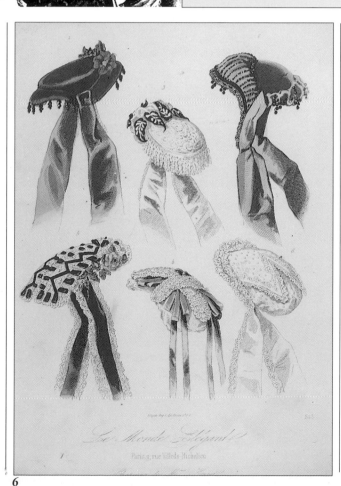

6

7

# DIAMONDS AND PEARLS

(1) *A six-row pearl necklace with an emerald and diamond clasp. As far as the Victorians were concerned, the more rows of pearls one could muster, the better.* (2) *A portrait on porcelain of Queen Victoria, after the watercolour by Franz Xavier Winterhalter, favourite portraitist of Europe's jewel-bedecked royalty.*

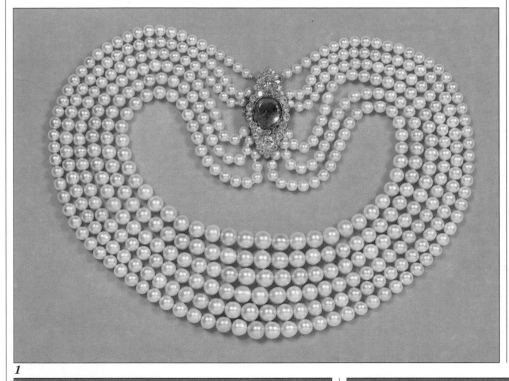

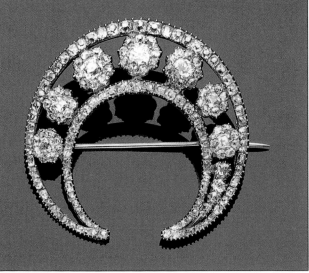

(3) *A diamond and pearl star of the type that could be worn as a hair ornament or as a brooch, and* (4) *a diamond-studded crescent brooch, useful for gathering swathes of lace, or for adorning the hair.*

1

2

3

4

5

6

7

*(5) A delicately looped pearl and diamond necklace in the Rococo style; (6) a Rococo-inspired pearl and diamond brooch, and (7) a cluster of Victorian diamond brooches and earrings: bows were among the favourite motifs in the 1890s.*

# ARCHAEOLOGICAL JEWELLERY

*(1)* A mid-19th-century gold pendant inspired by the jewellery designs of Hans Holbein, and *(2)* a Renaissance-style enamelled pendant set with rubies, pearls and diamonds by Carlo Giuliano.

**3**

**4**

*(3)* A group of Italian hardstone cameo jewels carved with classical heads, dating from mid-century. The flower-framed onyx suite (bracelet, brooch and earrings) and the hinged "archaeological" bangle are carved from three layers of stone to maximize natural colouring. The carver of the unmounted onyx cameo on the right has made subtle use of four striations of colour, while the left-hand portrait of Dante is of two shades of agate. *(4)* A malachite cross and earrings inset with micro-mosaic flowers, birds and insects.

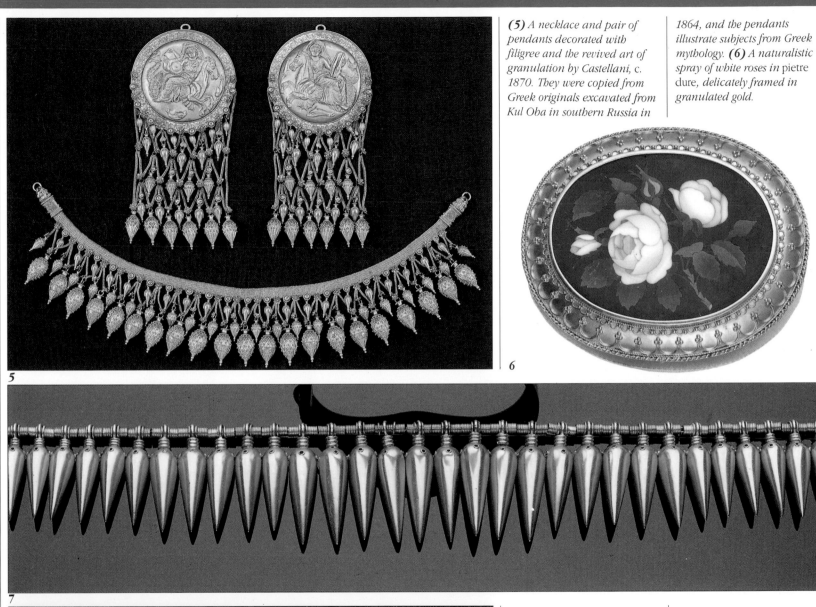

*(5)* A necklace and pair of pendants decorated with filigree and the revived art of granulation by Castellani, c. 1870. They were copied from Greek originals excavated from Kul Oba in southern Russia in 1864, and the pendants illustrate subjects from Greek mythology. *(6)* A naturalistic spray of white roses in pietre dure, delicately framed in granulated gold.

*(7)* A mid-19th-century necklace in the Etruscan style, with graduated amphora-shaped drops hanging from a reeded chain. The simplicity of such pieces belies the craftsmanship involved in making them, and they provide interesting contrasts with the showily elaborate jewels more often associated with the Victorian period. *(8)* A Gothic-style gold and champlevé enamel headband set with a ruby and turquoises, designed by A.W.N. Pugin and made by John Hardman & Co. of Birmingham in 1848.

*A pewter hot water jug with a cane handle, designed by Archibald Knox for Liberty's Tudric range, 1904.*

# CHAPTER SIX
# SILVER
# AND
# METALWORK

During the Victorian era the silver trade flourished as never before. The development of machine processes resulted in new techniques and easier and cheaper production, allowing many more people to buy. Silver had irresistible appeal for an aspiring middle class looking for outward and visible signs of wealth and prestige. The result was an unprecedented outpouring of decorative silver and silver-plate — cast, chased, embossed, turned and engraved — from manufacturers mostly based in London, Birmingham and Sheffield. Other established silver-producing cities — Dublin, Exeter, Chester and Edinburgh — continued, but on a small scale compared with the highly industrialized output of the three major centres.

In 1840 the Birmingham firm of Elkington patented a method of electro-plating and electro-gilding, and began systematically to buy up rival patents in silver-plating processes. This gave Elkington's a virtual monopoly over the silver-plating industry. Other firms could only use the "Electro Process" by licence, and several, notably Christofle of Paris, Barnard Bros. of London and Dixons of Sheffield, paid large sums for the privilege of coating objects made from an alloy of copper, tin and nickel with a thin skin of silver by this electrical process.

The resulting product was known as EPNS (electro-plated nickel silver) or EPGS (electro-plated German

*(1) A plated set of 12 cake spoons and a cake slice, with gilt blades, c. 1900. The ivy-leaf decoration and its sinuous framework are typical manifestations of popularized Art Nouveau. (2) A silver-mounted claret jug with wheel-engraved floral decoration on the glass and an elaborate concoction of Rococo motifs embossed on the metalwork, made by William Comyns, London, 1899.*

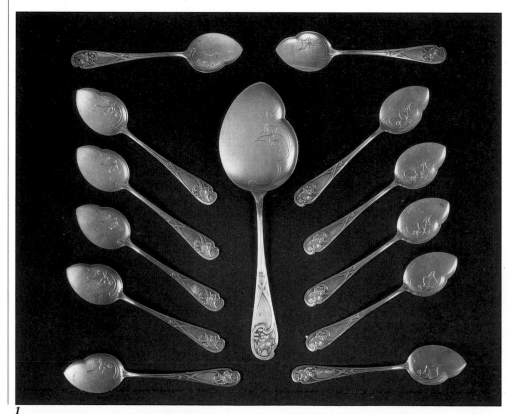

2

silver). Britannia metal, a silver substitute resembling pewter, invented in the 18th century, could also be electro-plated, and was known as EPBM. This new process was much less laborious than the old method of Sheffield plating, in which a layer of silver was fused to a layer of alloy (copper, zinc and lead) to form sheets of metal which could then be made into objects. By about 1850 electro-plating had almost entirely superseded Sheffield plate, and because it was relatively inexpensive it reached a whole new market. Later, in 1845, Elkington's introduced electro-typing, by which metal could be electrically deposited within a mould, and this meant that all kinds of articles of any material — even plants — could be exactly reproduced.

### Presentation silver

The apogee of high Victorian silver is to be seen in the period's many presentation pieces, given to commemorate personal events like baptisms and marriages, or in

1

recognition of long service and spectacular achievements. They ranged from massive table centrepieces and ornate trophies to candlesticks, inkstands and mugs. Vast quantities of small items and toys were also produced in response to the Victorian thirst for ornament and novelty. The period's many exhibitions gave rise to elaborate and impractical *tours de force* of Victorian eclecticism, of astonishing craftsmanship but appalling vulgarity.

The reaction away from the severe Classicism of the early 19th century towards the romantic and undisciplined Rococo can be seen in silver as early as the 1820s, when a trend towards the massive was already established. Traditional silver shapes were loaded with applied ornament such as asymmetrical scrolls, leaves, shells or chinoiseries. The results bore little resemblance to the stylish and light-hearted Rococo of the 18th century, but that was not the point. The Rococo style was perceived as giving maximum opportunity for decorative efects, and as for most Victorians ornament equalled art, the more that could be crammed onto a single item the more artistic that item must be. Rococo decoration was even hammered into 18th-century teapots or bowls.

Not only Rococo, but Renaissance, Baroque, Gothic and Classical styles were adopted for silver, sometimes with archaeological precision, but more often in the confusing *mélange* of ornamental forms. As a contemporary lamented in the *Journal of Design* in 1849: "There is no general agreement in the principle of taste . . . we all agree only in being imitators."

The inspiration of 16th-century goldsmith Benvenuto Cellini was cited as the basis for much of the Renaissance revival silver of the mid-19th century. Although very few actual examples of his work were known, silver was decorated with masks, strapwork and Mannerist motifs or with cast Classical figures in what was thought to be his style.

Pugin designed silver and brass in the "pointed Christian style", first for the influential firm of Rundell, Bridge & Rundell and later for John Hardman & Co, the ecclesiastical metalworkers of Birmingham; others sprinkled Gothic motifs about their metallic homages to the "olden time".

Naturalistic subjects, in tune with the Rococo, were always the most popular. Early on in the period silversmiths were much influenced by the works of Frederick Knight, whose pattern books for metalworkers included *Knight's Scroll Ornaments* (c.1830) and *Knight's Vases and Ornaments*. Scrolling plants and acanthus leaves, basketwork, flowers and allegorical figures were applied to all kinds of objects. Naturalism was carried a stage further in such novelties as inkwells shaped like waterlilies or medieval gargoyles, condiment sets in the form of owls or monkeys, beehive honeypots, shell butter dishes, apple-shaped teapots and goat cream jugs.

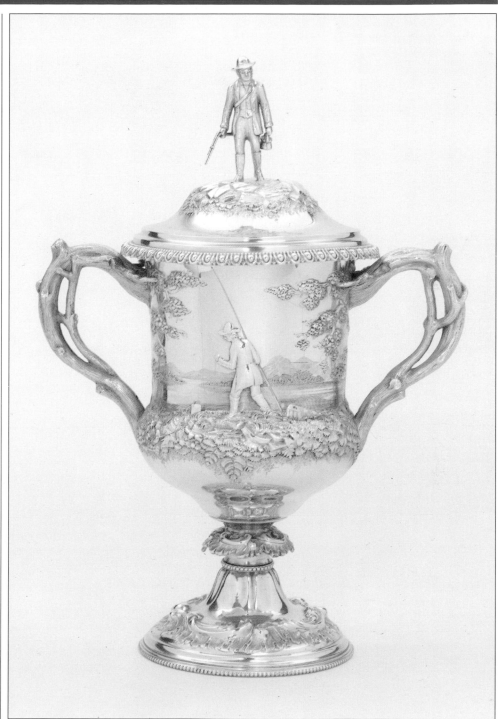

**3**

*(3) A silver cup and cover with rustic handles by James Dixon & Son of Sheffield, 1859-60. The maker of this high-quality sporting trophy, although giving* it wholly appropriate chased decoration and Neo-Classical shape, was unable to resist Rococo flourishes in the base.*

*(1) Chinese (and Rococo) influence is to be seen in this tea and coffee service with its floral repoussé chasing and Chinamen finials. It was made by the London makers Bateman & Ball in 1842.*

*1*

### Mass production

Quality of workmanship varied rather less than quality of design. While some mass-produced silver was thin and shoddy, particularly towards the end of the century, most was sturdily made, and there can be little doubt of the Victorian silversmiths' skill in casting and chasing.

Some firms, such as that of the Fox family, Garrards, and Hunt & Roskell produced large pieces of outstanding workmanship, while the smallworkers of Birmingham such as Nathaniel Mills, Joseph Willmore and others made boxes and toys of exquisite precision. Almost all maintained high standards of craftsmanship; it was the design that brought such strong criticism.

Efforts to improve public taste were launched by such organizations as the Art Union and the Royal Society of Arts, while the Select Committee on Arts and Manufactures had been set up by Parliament as early as 1835, in an attempt to raise artistic standards in manufacturing. But while these laudable efforts did result in sporadic outbreaks of decoration suited to purpose, silver was one of the last of the decorative arts to fall under the purifying influence of the Arts and Crafts Movement.

Its most radical reformer was Christopher Dresser, whose designs for the Birmingham firm of Hukin & Heath in the 1880s must have astounded even progressive Victorians with their bold modernity. He also designed silver and plated wares for James Dixon of Sheffield and Elkington of Birmingham.

Some time before this, the Japanese influence had arrived. From the 1870s firms such as Barnard Bros. and Elkington produced tea-wares and other pieces decorated with the same oriental motifs — birds, fans, blossoms, willow trees, sunbursts and fretwork — that were to be seen on aesthetic furniture. Shapes as well as decorative themes were soon affected, particularly after Christopher Dresser had visited Japan in 1877 to study Japanese arts and to collect artefacts for Tiffany in New York and for the South Kensington Museum in London. These gave inspiration to designers of the 1880s on both sides of the Atlantic, while silver was among the imported Japanese wares on sale in Liberty's from 1875.

The Arts and Crafts ideal of honest functionalism is best exemplified in the work of C.R. Ashbee. In 1888 he founded the Guild of Handicraft, an association of like-minded artist-craftsmen which survived until 1907. His own work in silver relied on simple forms, many derived from the Gothic, and he relished such evidence of hand-work as hammer marks on the surface. Drawn wire handles and mouldings were typical, and many of his pieces were decorated with inlays of semi-precious stones or enamels. When Liberty's introduced their Cymric silver and Tudric pewter in 1899, these hammered surfaces were produced by machine.

By the turn of the century, Liberty's were purveying Art Nouveau instead of "Japonisme", and their Cymric and Tudric ranges were inspired by Celtic ornament as well as the work of Ashbee and the Guild of Handicraft. The designer Archibald Knox is always associated with Liberty metalwork of this period, but others were also involved, including Rex Silver (son of Arthur, founder of the Silver Studios) and Jessie M. King. Many of the pieces were manufactured by the Birmingham firm of W.H. Haseler.

But the progressive forms of the Arts and Crafts Movements and Art Nouveau appealed to a small minority. The mass of the population continued to cling to safer historical revivals and reproductions, and manufacturers found a receptive market for their "Queen Anne", "Adam" and "Louis-Quinze" imitation pieces, as well as for accurate replicas.

### Base metals

Base metals enjoyed a revival in the 1870s and 1880s: iron and copper as well as pewter were used for decorative motifs, hinges and handles on progressive furniture, as well as for domestic items. A leader in the design and production of artistic metalwork was W.A.S. Benson, an associate of William Morris. He produced an array of practical items, including light fittings in copper, brass and iron, from his factory in Hammersmith; they were sold in his own shop in Bond Street and in Bing's Maison de l'Art Nouveau in Paris.

Benson also made designs for cast-iron grates and fireplaces. Most of these were carried out at the Coalbrookdale Ironworks, long established as a leading foundry for all kinds of cast iron — structural metalwork, garden furniture, utility items like footscrapers, doorknockers and umbrella stands, statuary and small decorative pieces. Other important foundries supplying the vast domestic market included Carron of Falkirk, Kenrick, and Barnard, Bishop & Barnard of Norwich.

*(2) A silver-plated toast rack with a screw-opening receptacle in the bottom for hot water, a stylishly simple and practical design dating from 1890. (3) An electroplated tea set designed by Christopher Dresser and probably made by James Dixon & Co.,* c. 1880.

2

3

Barnard, Bishop & Barnard are best known for their connection with the architect Thomas Jeckyll, who made designs for cast iron in the Gothic style in the 1860s, and later became one of the outstanding exponents of the Anglo-Japanese taste. His cast- and wrought-iron Japanese pavilion was shown in the Philadelphia Centennial Exhibition in 1876 and in the Paris Exhibition in 1878.

A significant visual contribution to the Victorian interior was made by the japanned metalwares of Wolverhampton and Birmingham. The art of japanning in

Europe was originally developed in the 17th century as a substitute for the exotic and expensive lacquered ware of the Orient, and was later applied to metals and papier mâché. By the Victorian period a considerable industry for japanned wares — both papier mâché and tin-plate — was well established in the West Midlands. Items such as trays, plate-warmers, coal boxes, tea caddies, snuff boxes, inkstands and candlesticks were produced in the full range of Victorian decorative styles.

# INSPIRATIONS

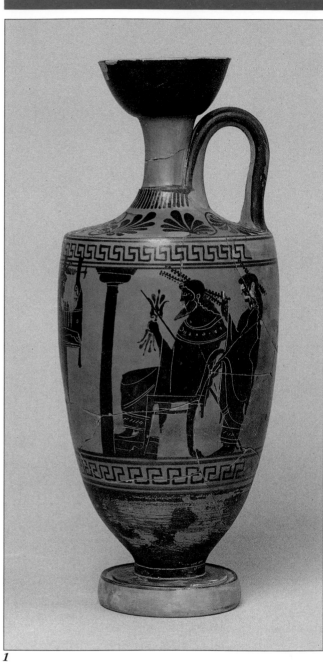

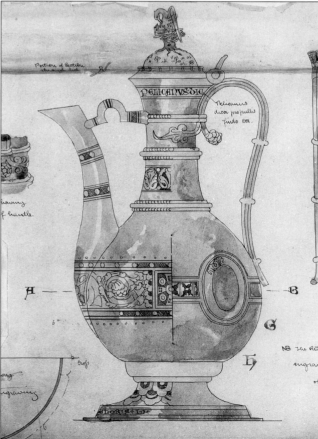

*(1)* Both the shapes and decorative motifs of ancient Greek pots such as this Greek amphora were translated into metalwork during the 19th century. *(4)* William Burges's design for a flagon for the church of St Michael and All Angels, Brighton, later made in silver by Charles Hart in 1862.

Burges was a respected authority on metalwork as well as a passionate medievalist, and through the Ecclesiological Society he exerted considerable influence on the design of both church and secular plate.

*(2)* The Newdigate Centrepiece by Paul de Lamerie (1743-44). Silver such as this appealed to the Victorians' sense of show: they enthusiastically copied Rococo forms and decorative elements. *(3)* Detail from a print by the Japanese artist Hokusai, c. 1840. From the 1860s, when quantities of Japanese art flowed into Europe, a fresh freedom as well as a new vocabulary of motifs was evident.

*(6) Celtic designs from Owen Jones's* Grammar of Ornament. *The interlacing patterns of the Celts were used by many of the Gothic revivalists long before they inspired designers like Archibald Knox. (7) An illustration of the reliquary of St Edmund by A.W.N. Pugin, 1832. Pugin's powerful influence on the course of the Victorian Gothic revival was largely due to his own intense studies: he travelled widely, sketching and collecting wherever he went.*

5

*(5) A drawing of a pectoral worked in gold and jewels designed by the Medici Pope Clement VII and made by the 16th-century goldsmith Benvenuto Cellini, whose name was invoked in connection with countless Victorian Renaissance revivals. In fact very little goldsmithing could be ascribed to Cellini with certainty, and it was not until 1898 that C.R. Ashbee's translation of his* Treatise on Goldsmithing and Sculpture *was published.*

6

RELIQVARY which belonged to St E

# SHOW PIECES

(1) A cast silver-gilt épergne with shell-shaped dishes of striped glass and an elaborate flower finial, in the high Victorian Rococo style, made by Robert Garrard c. 1865.

**1**

**2**

(2) A two-handled silver bowl with repoussé decorations of naturalistic roses, by Gilbert Marks, London, 1897. Like other silversmiths in the Arts and Crafts tradition, Marks combined the roles of artist, designer and craftsman in his distinctive hand-made pieces, no two of which were the same.
(3) A cast and finely chiselled gilt bronze candelabrum in the neo-Greek style by Ferdinand Barbedienne, 1862. A leading Parisian bronze-founder, Barbedienne was associated with many of the period's best known artists and sculptors.

**3**

4

*(4) An oxidized silver casket with cast and repoussé decoration made by Rudolphi of Paris and exhibited, among his works of art in silver, gold, precious and semi-precious stones and enamels, at the Great Exhibition of 1851.*

*(6) A silver cup and cover with a blue and green enamelled wave pattern round the bowl, designed by Archibald Knox for Liberty's Cymric silver range, 1900. At the time it was described as a "Presentation or Challenge Cup".*

*(5) A late 19th-century Dutch or German silver nef in the form of a fully rigged 16th-century sailing ship. The nef, originally used "for the lord's napkin, knife and spoon" — or for salt — on the aristocratic medieval table, was revived during the Victorian period as a status enhancing table decoration.*

5

6

# BASE METALS

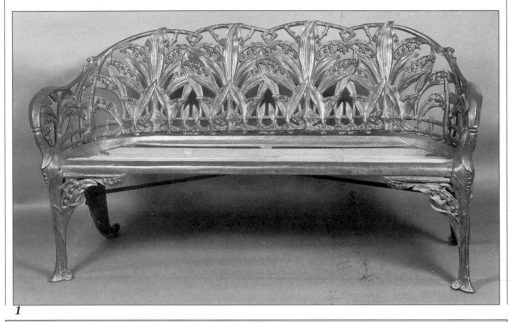

(1) *A mid-19th-century cast-iron garden seat with a pattern of lily of the valley, made at the Coalbrookdale Ironworks, the leading English foundry for ornamental cast iron.*

**1**

**2**

## JAPANNED TINWARES

Birmingham and Wolverhampton were the chief centres of production for both japanned tin and papier mâché wares, some firms such as Walton & Co. and Henry Loveridge & Co. of Wolverhampton, produced both. Victorian japanned tin products included such items as plate-warmers, coal boxes, tea caddies, snuffboxes, inkstands and candlesticks in the full range of the period's style. However, just as with papier mâché production, trays of all shapes and sizes predominated. This example, dating from *circa* 1865, of round "Gothic" shape, is painted with a still life of fruit, apple blossom and scrolled acanthus-leaf border in

two shades of gold leaf. The painting is the work of Richard Stubbs and the gilding that of Edwin Stubbs, both working for Henry Loveridge, It is typical of the fine work, akin to enamelling on porcelain, that is to be found among the best examples of 19th-century japanning.

The jappaned tin industry declined after the 1850s, largely overtaken by the success of electro-plated wares, and papier mâché was not slow to follow. Only a few firms survived into the 20th century.

(2) *Barnard, Bishop & Barnard's pavilion at the Centennial Exhibition, Philadelphia, 1876. This lavish foray into the Japanese taste was made by the Norwich firm of ornamental ironworkers, and designed by Thomas Jeckyll, as were the wrought-iron firedogs (3), made by Barnard, Bishop & Barnard. Jeckyll was the leading exponent of the aesthetic taste in metalwork, and the sunflower was his personal leitmotiv.*

**3**

*(5) A beaten copper firehood by M.H. Baillie Scott, in the study at White Lodge, Wantage. Baillie Scott's designs owe a debt to both Mackmurdo and Knox and, like Voysey, he was at the forefront of English influence on domestic architecture abroad. (6) A detail of the brass doors leading to the chamber of the House of Lords, designed by A.W.N. Pugin and made, like most of Pugin's metalwork, by John Hardman & Co. of Birmingham.*

*(4) A cast-iron fountain made at the Coalbrookdale Ironworks. Besides garden statuary and furniture the firm produced architectural ironwork such as firegrates and mantelpieces as well as furnishings like door knockers, umbrella stands, chairs, tables and even ornamental dishes with pierced decoration.*

# TECHNIQUES AND MATERIALS

**(2)** *A silver teapot, milk jug and lidded sugar basin in the aesthetic taste, with elaborately moulded handles and finials, engraved bullrushes and bamboo, and applied herons, kingfishers and butterflies. The set was made by the Goldsmiths' Alliance, London, 1880.*

**1**

**(1)** *A rock crystal, gold and enamel bowl, c. 1870 by the Parisian jeweller Alexis Falize. The various techniques of enamelling were explored by many 19th-century designers, especially towards the end of the century. Here* cloisonné *enamelling, in which the pigments are confined in little cells (*cloisons*), is used around the rim, with* pliqué-à-jour *enamelled panels below. This is a technique of even greater intricacy, in which the background metal is removed after firing to reveal the* enamel's translucency. The inside is lined with medieval hunting scenes in champlevé enamelling, in which the metal around the design is scooped out and filled with colour. **(3)** An electro-plated pie dish with a broody hen cover, by G.R. Collis and Co. circa 1875. Collis was one of several firms who used the technique patented by George Elkington for decorative metalwork. His method of covering metal with a thin layer of silver by electrical deposition led to the demise of the Sheffield plate industry.

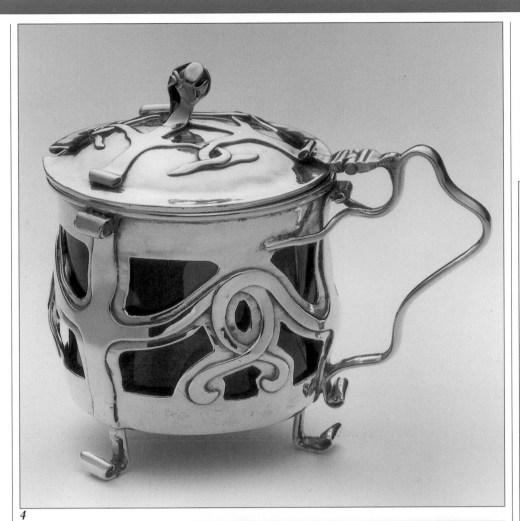

4

*(4)* *A silver mustard pot with applied intertwining strapwork in the characteristically organic Arts and Crafts style, signed "E.B.", and made in Birmingham in 1902.*

6

*(5)* *A late 19th-century enamelled bowl showing the jewel-like translucency of colour that could be achieved with the* pliqué-à-jour *technique.*

5

*(6)* *A pewter clock with enamelled face, made for Liberty, c. 1900. The hand-crafted appearance of beaten pewter and the smooth polished look seen in this piece were both fashionable in the Art Nouveau period.*

3

1

*(3) An Art Nouveau pewter tea service with relief decorations designed by Hugo Leven for Kayser Sohn of Krefeld, 1900. Leven's metalwork was imported and sold by Liberty, and was influential on the designs of Archibald Knox.*

*(1) A pewter tobacco jar with a stylized honesty pattern, designed by Archibald Knox for Liberty's Tudric range, and (2) a brass teapot, c. 1896, by C.F.A. Voysey, whose simple organic style was equally satisfying in architecture,* *wallpaper, furniture or metalwork. Voysey's designs were enormously influential on the development of Art Nouveau on the Continent, although he himself disliked the style.*

4

5

6

(4) A painted copper, brass and wood candlestick designed by Christopher Dresser and made by Perry and Co. 1883. A prolific designer of metalwork, ceramics, glass, furniture, textiles and wallpapers, Dresser was one of the few to be in sympathy both with the principles of the Arts and Crafts Movement and with the needs of machine production. (6) An inkwell of silver with panels of enamelled lilies, by C.R. Ashbee for the Guild of Handicraft. Ashbee was instrumental in founding this co-operative group of craftsmen in 1888, and their work was regularly exhibited in the Arts and Crafts Exhibitions.

(5) A pair of candlesticks, c. 1860, by Philip Webb, one of the leaders, with William Morris, of the Arts and Crafts Movement. He is perhaps best known as an architect, notably of The Red House for Morris, but his designs also included stained glass, embroidery, jewellery, metalwork, furniture and lettering.

# REPRESENTATIONAL

**(1)** *A bronze figure of a Bacchante,* c. *1860, stamped Clodion. The subtly erotic terracotta figures of the late 18th-century French sculptor, Claude Michel Clodion, were immensely popular with the Victorians, who copied them in bronze as well as terracotta. Most are of pastoral or classical subjects and are often stamped with his name even when made long after his death.*

1

2

**(2)** *A silver vinaigrette of the type known as a "castle top". This one, showing Warwick Castle, was made in Birmingham* c. *1840.*

**(3)** *A pair of bronze equestrian portrait groups, c. 1870, by Alfred Emile O'Hara, Comte de Nieuwerkerke and Jacques-Auguste Fauginet, cast by the Paris firm of Susse Frères. They are typical of the* bronzes d'ameublement, *sometimes issued in limited edition, which enjoyed enormous popularity* in the furnishing of the Victorian home.

**(4)** *A silver mustard pot in the form of an owl, its spoon finished with a mouse terminal. This combination of humour and fine craftsmanship was made in London in 1866 by George Richards and Edward Charles Brown.*

**(6)** *A cold-painted bronze figure of an Arab holding up a carpet, c. 1900, of the type produced in Vienna by Franz Bergman. His scenes of Arabian life often included carpets painted in realistic detail.*

3   4

**(5)** *A table lighter-cum-match-holder in the form of a standing bear, by J.B. Hennell, London 1876. The silversmithing firm of Hennell, established in the 1730s, maintained its reputation for good craftsmanship throughout the 19th century, and survives to this day.*

5

6

153

*A stoneware vase, 30.5cm (12in) high,
dated 1888, and decorated by E.
Bennett at C.J.C. Bailey's Fulham*

# CHAPTER SEVEN
# CERAMICS AND GLASS

Industrialization of the pottery industry, well advanced by the 1830s, not only allowed greater quantities of pottery and porcelain to be produced than ever before, but gave an unprecedented degree of control over the material. Clays were more refined, kilns and firing processes more predictable, glazes and colours more varied. This freedom from the expensive uncertainties that had dogged so much 18th-century production cleared the way for the enormous surge of technical and artistic development that took place at a time when the new railways were making distribution more efficient.

The design of ceramics was affected as much by individuals as it was by techniques, fashions and revivals. There were factory owners of outstanding enterprise like Herbert Minton and William Taylor Copeland. Artists, many of them immigrants from the Continent, introduced new styles and techniques. Men of science, experimenting with glazes and bodies, widened the scope of decoration and shape. The achievements of the 19th-century ceramicists can be seen at their most flamboyantly confident in the many exhibitions of the period: ostentatious they may have been, unadventurous they were not.

### Sèvres and Rococo

The major influence on porcelain decoration at the beginning of the period came from Sèvres in France, whose museum was an important repository of historical

2

types and whose director in the first half of the 19th century was a great technical pioneer, Alexandre Brogniart. The taste for collecting antique pieces (*vieux Sèvres*) prompted a blooming of Sèvres-style flower decoration on English porcelain, particularly at Minton and Coalport, and a misleadingly named *Rose du Barry* pink ground. But the technical developments at Sèvres in the middle years of the century did get taken up later in England largely thanks to French immigrant ceramists working in English factories.

Inspiration for the Rococo revival in ceramics came partly from silver and partly from Meissen and its many imitators in eastern Europe, whose decorative wares were generally imported under the blanket label "Dresden". In any case, the Rococo style was well suited both to the bone china body now standard in England and to industrial production.

Some figure groups were based closely on 18th-century originals, but the majority of pieces, flower-encrusted and of *bombe* form, were only loosely derived. "Rococo" scrolls, cartouches, asymmetrical flowers and

1

plants, relief ornament and gilding gave full rein to decorators, and English porcelain manufacturers adopted it with enthusiasm.

### Revival styles

In transfer-printed earthenwares historical revivalism was also rife, but relief decoration was generally confined to the borders of plates, or to moulded panels on jugs and vessels. Topographical or fanciful scenes, or flower subjects, were often bordered with elaborate patterns in the Rococo, Gothic or Chinese taste.

Besides traditional blue, the colours black, green, brown, red, purple and yellow were introduced by the Victorians, and by the late 1840s, a method of multi-colour printing on earthenware had been developed by Felix Pratt of Fenton and the artist Jesse Austin. Other Staffordshire firms soon copied, and polychrome printing was used for tablewares and for potlids, many of which had an advertising function.

Moulded decoration can be seen in revivalist variety on the slip-cast jugs of the 1840s and 1850s. Classical revivalism also extended to Wedgwood's jasper decora-tion, and to a range of red and black unglazed earthen-ware decorated with "Etruscan" or "Etrurian" figure subjects and stylized borders, made among others by Copeland, Dillwyn of Swansea and F & R Pratt of Fenton. Persian and "Moresque" decoration was sometimes a careful reproduction of early examples to be seen in the new public museums, and sometimes a free adaptation of Islamic motifs.

The Renaissance period gave inspiration to a number of types. Minton followed the mid-century lead of several potters in France in making "Palissy" wares, imitating the high-relief, brightly glazed confections of plants, shells, snakes and lizards originally conceived by the 16th-century French potter Bernard Palissy.

Worcester's speciality, "Limoges" ware, painted by the artist Thomas Bott in white enamel on a dark blue ground, was directly inspired by Prince Albert's own collection of 16th-century Limoges *grisaille*-painted enamels. Both Minton and Wedgwood copied the inlaid clay decoration known as Henri-Deux ware or Saint Porchaire, and Minton produced wares in the Italian maiolica style, some of them designed by Alfred Stevens.

*(3) Influenced by the painted earthenware of Theodore Deck and Emile Lessore, Doulton began to develop the production of similar wares at the Lambeth Studio in 1872. These three examples of Lambeth faience were decorated by (left to right): Minna Crawley (1877) Euphemia Thatcher (c. 1882) and Kate Rogers (c. 1892).*

3

1

"Majolica" was the name the Victorians gave to the popular pieces with relief decoration under brightly coloured glazes, first evolved by Leon Arnoux at Minton in imitation of Italian *maiolica* ware. Jardinières and vases, figures, dishes and decorative objects large and small were sculpted in colourful brilliance at Minton and other factories.

### Parian ware and fine art pottery

Parian ware — named because of its similarity to the finest Paros marble used by the ancient Greek sculptors — was a marble-like white biscuit porcelain developed for classical-style figures at Copeland's but used by Minton and others from the 1840s onwards. These were special designs or reduced versions of statues by some of the period's eminent sculptors, and many were commissioned by the Art Union or by Henry Cole as part of the drive to improve public taste. Reductions of large-scale sculpture became relatively simple after the invention of Cheverton's reducing machine, patented in 1844.

Individual designers and potters, many of them already reacting against the soulless technical excellence of industrial production, saw a new freedom in Japanese pottery. Earlier attempts to improve industrially produced ceramics by involving fine artists in their design were taken a stage further by the Arts and Crafts Movement, which promoted the value of individual artist-craftsmen and led to the flowering of studio pottery, with its bold shapes and experimental glazes.

A new vitality was apparent in "art pottery", much of it produced in small factories like those of Brannam in Devon, Bretby in Staffordshire, Brampton in Derbyshire, Elton in Somerset, the Della Robbia pottery of Birkenhead, or the Linthorpe pottery near Middlesbrough for which Christopher Dresser provided designs.

### New developments in glassmaking

Glass in Europe in the 1820s and 1830s was dominated by developments mainly in Bohemia and France. The exported results — hyalith and lithyalin, flashed and cased glass from Bohemia, and opaline from France — were eagerly snapped up in the British Isles, where manufacturers were at that time having to put up with a strait-jacket of excise duty and regulation which effectively prevented technical development and change. It was not until 1845 that the glass duty was finally abolished and British glassmaking could move in new directions.

The prevailing taste was for massiveness, whether the glass was cut or coloured. While the imported items were predominantly of strong rich colours or painted in enamels, cut clear glass had been an English speciality for a long time, and that produced during the 1830s and 1840s was of sturdy form and elaborate decoration.

The traditional centre of glassmaking in England was Stourbridge in Worcestershire, conveniently near to plentiful supplies of coal for the furnaces as well as to waterways for transport. The best-known names in 19th-century glass included the Stourbridge factories of Richardson, Webb, and Stevens & Williams. Newcastle-upon-Tyne, long established as a glassmaking centre, maintained its importance throughout the century. Among other major producers were Molineaux, Webb & Co of Manchester, Osler of Birmingham, James Powell & Sons of the Whitefriars Glassworks, London, Apsley Pellatt of Blackfriars, Chance, the sheet-glass specialist of Birmingham, and the Holyrood Flint Glass Works of Edinburgh.

Once duty had been taken off glass, British makers were at last able to compete with continental imports, and specialists from abroad were encouraged to come to

England and contribute their expertise to the ensuing outburst of innovation in both ornamental and utilitarian glass. Among the most significant developments was that of press-moulding, first pioneered in America, which made a whole range of mass-produced wares more cheaply available than before, and was to bring about a decline in cut glass after the 1850s. There was also an outpouring of coloured glass of every hue, as well as careful copies of Bohemian and French originals, while novelties included Varnish's patent double-walled silvered glass and Apsley Pellatt's cameos.

### Revival styles

Stylistically, glass was subject to the same historical revivals as other decorative arts. Campaigns by the Society of Arts and by Felix Summerly's Art Manufactures attempted to improve design for industry. The Great Exhibition was the culmination of these efforts, but the glass seen there emphasized the early Victorians' habitual lack of restraint in ornament while re-affirming their astonishing technical virtuosity.

Producers continued to furnish the market with elaborate cut, press-moulded or engraved clear glass, besides the continental-inspired novelties, many of which gave glass the appearance of other substances — porcelain, marble, rock crystal and even japanned tin.

For many of the artistic élite, it was Venetian glass, with its reliance on "fair colour, free grace of form, and artistic quality of material" (Ruskin), that was the focus of interest, and firms like James Powell supplied any gaps in the market unfilled by Salviati's imports.

### Cameos and etched glass

Of great economic and technical importance was the development of acid-etching on glass during the 1850s and 1860s. This took place in the Stourbridge area, at first at Richardson's factory and later in the workshops of one of their ex-employees, John Northwood. The use of hydrofluoric acid instead of the wheel for engraving was cheaper and at the same time gave opportunities for greater delicacy of decoration.

Hydrofluoric acid was also used in the making of cameo glass. This was a progression of cased glass, in which an outer layer of opaque white glass was filled with and fused to an inner contrasting colour. Unwanted areas of the outer casing were removed with acid to reveal the coloured body underneath, while the remaining white shape could be carved into sculptured relief. Cameo decoration was applied to useful wares as well as ornamental plaques and show pieces; backgrounds were often delicately tinted, with frosted surfaces. Later, in the 1880s and 1890s, cameo glass found its most celebrated exponents in the French Art Nouveau glassmakers Emile Gallé and the Daum brothers.

One of the most widely produced coloured varieties was ruby glass, known as cranberry in the United States. Some was embellished with illustrations of children in opaque white – "Mary Gregory decoration", so called after the artist who initiated the type at the Boston & Sandwich Glass Company in Massachussetts in the 1870s. She was widely copied, in central Europe as well as in America, at least until the 1920s. American influence was also seen in "Burmese" glass in which opaque pink and yellow tones were achieved with uranium oxide and gold, and in a number of other coloured varieties.

Acid-etched plate glass was used most strikingly in shops and pubs, whose doors and windows exhibited all the exuberance of Victorian popular design. Finally, the revival of stained glass work – initiated as part of the Gothic revival – meant that from the last decades of the century, stained glass panels embellished the doorways of grand mansions and humble terrace houses alike.

*(2) An opalescent and clear pressed glass butter dish of the type known as Holly Amber among collectors, but marketed as Golden Agate by the Indiana Tumbler & Goblet Company, Greentown, who made it.*

2

# INSPIRATIONS

*1*

*(1) A 16th-century Turkish (Isnik) white earthenware dish painted in underglaze colours. It was from such tin-glazed wares as this that William de Morgan drew inspiration for his tiles and decorative wares. (3) These three Bow porcelain figure groups represent (left to right):* Winter *and* Summer *from a set of the* Four Seasons *and* The Sailor's Return. *Flower-encrusted figures like these were the basis for the Rococo-style outpourings of many 19th-century porcelain producers.*

*(2) A glass lamp from the mosque of Sultan Hassan, Cairo, dated 1363. It is of a type copied by the Parisian glass worker Joseph Brocard in the 1870s.*

*2*

*3*

*(4)* Sèvres was a predominating influence on early Victorian porcelain, and many producers (including Sèvres themselves) tried to reproduce the highly prized soft-paste *vieux Sèvres porcelain of the 1856-74 period. This cashepôt of 1757, with a Rose Pompadour ground, is an example. (6)* The Pledge of Loyalty in the Peach Orchard, circa *1830, by the prolific Japanese printmaker Utagawa Kunisada. The impact of Japanese popular prints was apparent on all forms of design from the 1860s onwards.*

4

*(5)* Two medieval designs from Owen Jones's Grammar of Ornament. *Patterns similar to these were used for encaustic tiles, produced on a large scale from the 1840s after Herbert Minton had re-developed the medieval technique of inlaying clay slip of one colour into a plastic clay of a different colour.*

5

6

# STYLES FROM THE CONTINENT

(1) *A late 19th-century vase by Helena Wolfsohn of Dresden, a prolific reproducer of Meissen porcelain. Many of her products wre marked with the AR (Augustus Rex) monogram, which was not used on genuine Meissen after 1730, but she was eventually banned from using any Meissen mark.*

(2) *A flower-encrusted pot-pourri in the neo-Rococo style. It was made at Coalport, a leading factory for this type of decoration, whose popularity lasted throughout the Victorian period. Flower-encrusted porcelains had been produced at both Meissen and Sèvres during the 18th century.*

1

2

**3**

**(3)** *A Minton majolica wine cooler, 1856. Leon Arnoux, art director at Minton from 1849 until 1892, developed a range of decorative earthenwares with brightly coloured low-temperature glazes inspired by Italian maiolica. First exhibited in 1851, they became extremely popular and widely copied.*

**(5)** *Bone china vase in the Sèvres style made by Minton. This piece was exhibited at the London International Exhibition of 1862, and bears the mark in rare puce used only for ceramics shown at that exhibition.*

**(4)** *An enamelled earthenware dish modelled in relief with snakes, lizards, snails and plant forms, made by C.J. Landain of Tours and exhibited in the Exposition Universelle, Paris, 1855. Wares such as this, in imitation of the 16th-century French potter Bernard Palissy, were also copied in Portugal and at Minton's.*

**4**

**5**

163

# ART AND INDUSTRY

**(1)** *A pastille burner of c. 1840 decorated in a Japan pattern of blues and iron-red with gilding.* *It was made by the Staffordshire firm of C.J. Mason, best known for Mason's Patent Ironstone.*

1

**(2)** *A Minton parian vase of tinted body encrusted with white passion flowers and foliage in relief, 1854. Minton began producing parian ware in 1846 and issued their first* *parian catalogue in 1852. The dust-catching delicacy of such vessels as this was impractical even for the Victorians, and later a glazed parian was more often used.*

2

3

5

6

*(3)Belleek porcelain is characterized by its iridescent glaze over a thin parian body. Such wares, often of finely modelled shell or basket forms with encrusted flowers, were made at the Belleek Porcelain Factory in Northern Ireland, established in 1857. Similar porcelains were produced in several American factories between 1880 and 1900. (4)A Minton plaque painted by Emile Lessore, circa 1858. Lessore was one of several French ceramists to work in England, first at Minton's and later for Wedgwood. Some of his figure subjects are based on Old Master paintings, but he also made a speciality of freely drawn chubby cherubs.*

4

*(5)A circular bread plate decorated with coloured glazes and stained clays in the encaustic style, designed by A.W.N. Pugin and made by Minton circa 1850.*

*(6)A porcelain pot-pourri decorated with enamel colours and gilding in imitation of cloisonné enamels, a speciality of the Minton factory in the 1860s and '70s.*

165

# ART AND INDUSTRY

(1) *A Minton copy of a 16th-century Persian (Iznik) bottle decorated in the characteristic "Rhodian" palette. The red pigment was only achieved* *after many years of experiment. Pieces like this were displayed by Minton at the London International Exhibition of 1871.*

2

1

(2) *A parian porcelain pilgrim flask with pâte-sur-pâte decoration by Marc-Louis Solon, exhibited by Minton's at the Philadelphia Exhibition in 1876. The parian body was found to be eminently suitable* *for this difficult and time-consuming technique, in which successive coats of clay slip were built up on a coloured porcelain surface to form a cameo-like relief decoration. The method originated in* *China and was perfected at Sèvres by a number of artists including Marc-Louis Solon, who came to England after the Franco-Prussian War in 1870 and introduced it at Minton's.*

3

*(3) A pair of Royal Worcester porcelain vases (1872) by James Hadley, whose ivory-coloured vases with bronze relief decoration are among the most adventurous Japanese interpretations.*

*(4) A large Doulton faience vase painted with hollyhocks and butterflies by Florence Lewis, an artist at Doulton's Lambeth Studios from about 1875-1897.*

## THE ORIENTAL INFLUENCE

The Chinese and Japanese porcelains shown in this 19th-century illustration are typical of those imported in the later Victorian period. Oriental pottery and porcelain was influential in Europe throughout the century, but it was the novelty of Japanese imports from the 1860s that made the most impact. Factories such as Worcester (after 1863 known as the Worcester Royal Porcelain Company), used an ivory-toned body for decorative pieces of Japanese form, and included bronzing with gilding and colours for decoration. Many of these

pieces are similar to lacquer wares in appearance, while Minton produced colourful porcelains in

imitation of *cloisonné* enamels. Oriental ivory carving was imitated in the pierced wares of George Owen at Worcester.

The arrangement of ornament showed differences of a more fundamental kind: motifs were sparsely used, often without borders or frameworks, and Classical symmetry was abandoned. The Japanese influence resulted in a revolutionary approach to design on many levels.

4

# FIGURATIVE CERAMICS

**(1)** *A Staffordshire figure by John Lloyd Shelton, c. 1840, representing a character in opera or drama. By the early 19th century Burslem in* *Staffordshire was well established as a centre of production for figures and groups in the folk art tradition.*

**(2)** *A portrait figure of Queen Victoria, one of the century's favourite images. This one, of parian porcelain, was designed by William Henry Goss, who, after working as a modeller and designer for Copeland for a short period in the 1850s,* *opened his own factory in Stoke on Trent, producing parian portrait busts and decorative pieces in "ivory porcelain". Later, his heraldic souvenirs were to become immensely popular, ensuring his fame with succeeding generations.*

3

**(3)** *Heroes of the Crimean War were popular subjects for representation. Here, Admiral Sir James Dundas, the commander of naval operations in 1854, is seen with the accoutrements of battle.* **(4)** *Many Staffordshire figures were* exported to America, and appropriate subjects were produced for this market. These three groups depict popular American personalities from the stage and politics.

4

## FAIRINGS

The small brightly coloured hard-paste porcelain figure groups known as fairings often reveal a surprisingly bawdy side of Victorian popular culture. Given away as prizes or bought for a few pence at fairs, their subjects range from "The last in bed to put out the light" or "Shall we sleep first, or how?" to macabre scenes of tooth-pulling, as in "A long pull and strong pull" and sporting subjects. Most deal with courtship, marriage or domestic life, and some, depicting a partially dressed maid

in a compromising situation, are decidedly risqué.

Despite the English inscriptions

with which they are almost invariably captioned — in black or gilt — fairings were made in

Germany by the firm of Conta & Bohme. Some of the subjects have been traced to English comic papers of the 1860s and 70s. It is likely that these were suggested to the manufacturers by the English importers, but some fairings display a barely concealed Germanic sense of humour.

# THE ART POTTERS

**(1)** *A William de Morgan ruby lustre dish painted with a galleon. De Morgan, an associated of William Morris, was one of the outstanding figures in the Arts and Crafts movement. Much of his* *inspiration came from Persia, and his experiments led to a revival of lustre techniques. His predominantly blue and green plant- and animal-decorated tiles and wares are equally distinctive.*

1

2

**(2)** *A ruby lustre plaque made at the Burmantofts Pottery near Leeds, one of a number of small firms producing high-quality art pottery in the 1880s and 1890s.*

## MARTINWARE

The most extraordinary of all studio pottery was that made from 1873 to 1914 by the Martin Brothers — Robert Wallace, Walter, Edwin and Charles, at first in Fulham and later in Southall. Using a grey stoneware, they modelled vases, jugs and other vessels in the form of grotesque birds, animals and fishes with bluish glazes and incised surface details. They also produced simpler forms such as Gothic-inspired candlesticks and clock cases, flower-embellished vases, in the Japanese taste and jugs incised with Baroque ornament.

The fish-form jug shown here is a characteristic piece of Martinware, most of which was designed by Wallace Martin. He had been trained as a sculptor and had worked for Doulton before setting up the Martin Brothers pottery.

(3) *An earthenware vase made at the Barnstaple pottery of Charles Brannam, who supplied Liberty with art pottery from 1882 until the late 1930s. The decoration is by W.L. Baron.* (4) *A pottery case decorated with a Persian-inspired design in shades of brown, 1887, by Maw and Co. one of the largest manufacturers of tiles in Britain. From about 1875, they also produced a range of art pottery.*

4

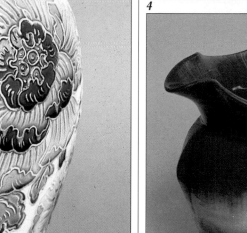

5

(5) *An earthenware jardinière decorated in the sang de boeuf (ox blood) glaze popular towards the end of the 19th century. It was made at the Bretby Art Pottery, Staffordshire, established in 1883, whose wares were described by a contemporary as "extremely quaint and artistic".*

3

# THE ART POTTERS

1

(1) *A salt-glaze Lambeth ware biscuit barrel with a silver lid and handle and decoration by Hannah Barlow, 1882. Henry Doulton's link with Lambeth School of Art from 1866 was a notable example of collaboration between art and industry and an important milestone in the art pottery revival. Hannah Barlow, the first female artist to be engaged by Doulton, worked at the studio for 42 years and specialized in incised designs of animals and birds, many of them inspired by her own private zoo.*

(2) *A salt-glaze Doulton ware jug 22.9cm (9in.) high, decorated in a swirling design of incised foliage and applied white beads and flowerheads. Such pieces were the "relaxation" of George Tinworth, the "untrained genius" of the Lambeth Studio, whose sculptured panels and small figures of mice, frogs and children are most distinctive.*

2

(3) *A late 19th-century vase from the Rookwood Pottery, Ohio, one of the most important* *of the many art potteries established in America in the 1880s.*

3

4

5

(4) *Two salt-glazed vases by Mark Marshall, one of Doulton's most gifted stoneware modellers, who worked for the Martin Brothers before joining Doulton's in 1880. Dragons,* *lizards and grotesque creatures were characteristic of his work.* (5) *Three Elton ware vases with lustre and metallic craquelure decoration. From the Sunflower Pottery, which he established in* *the 1880s at his home, Clevedon Court, Somerset, Sir Edmund Elton produced a range of highly individual art pottery decorated with coloured slips and lead glazes.*

# CERAMIC TILES

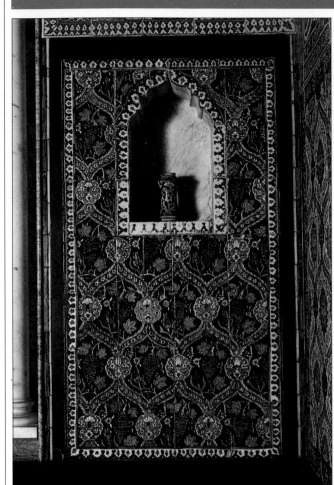

(3, 4, 5, 6) Spring, Summer, Autumn *and* Winter — *a set of tiles with hand-coloured designs of children representing the* Four Seasons *in the manner of Kate Greenaway, surrounded by blue and white transfer-printed borders in the Japanese-influenced aesthetic taste. They were made by the Staffordshire firm of T. & R. Boote, 1881.*

*(1) A* mihrab *(or prayer niche) in the Arab Hall at Leighton House, London, which was decorated with antique Islamic tiles complemented by tiles of similar blue/green hues designed by William de Morgan. (2) A tile picture of the Doulton Factory, Lambeth, from across the Thames, designed by John Eyre and painted by Esther Lewis, c. 1885. Tile pictures like this, in the Dutch tradition, were used a great deal in the Victorian period for commercial decoration, for example in pubs and butchers' shops.*

1

2

3

4

(7) Tiles were widely used for architectural decoration both inside and out. Here both Greek and Persian motifs can be seen in the ceramic facings of a railway building at Shrub Hill Station, Worcester, 1865.

7

8

(8) Four transfer-printed floral tiles of the 1870-80 period. The two upper examples have hand-coloured details added to the basic brown transfer print. Japanese influence can be seen in the composition of blossoms and waterlilies (bottom left), in the bordering fans of the pink-printed tile (bottom right) and in the rising sun and sunflower motif of the circular design (top right).

5

6

# GLASS TECHNIQUES

## CLUTHA GLASS

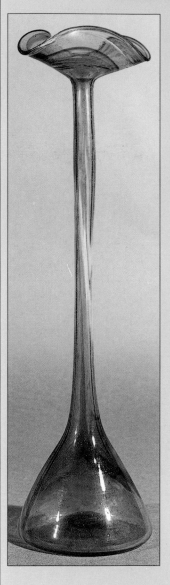

Towards the end of the century, a number of progressive designers exploited the ductile qualities of glass in adventurous ways, and by chemical experiment opened up new horizons of colour and texture. Christopher Dresser and George Walton's Clutha glass, made by James Couper & Sons of Glasgow during the 1880s and 1890s, featured the natural imperfections of glass. The simple if quirky forms of Clutha glass, as well as tinted colouring and the presence of streaks and bubbles, evoke ancient Roman and Middle Eastern originals. In America, Louis Comfort Tiffany produced Favrile glass, of colourful iridescence and graceful Art Nouveau shapes, similar to the products of Continental firms such as Lötz of Bohemia.

The plant-like form of this Clutha vase, nearly 43cm (17in.) high, is a reminder of Christopher Dresser's continuing interest in botany while at the same time embodying the organic flowing quality of Art Nouveau design.

1

*(1) A late-19th-century iridescent glass vase by Lötz (Witwe) of Klostemuble, Bohemia. The director of this firm, Max von Spaun, patented a method of iridizing glass in 1873. His products, exported to America during the 1880s, were undoubtedly influential on Tiffany's development of Favrile glass. (2) A vase decorated with engraved and enamelled moths by Emile Gallé, Nancy (1885-90). Gallé was a passionate botanist, and he used plant forms in much of his work. In this vase he was clearly looking towards Japan, but inspiration for his glass also came from Venetian and Islamic enamelled glass.*

2

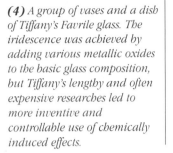

*(4) A group of vases and a dish of Tiffany's Favrile glass. The iridescence was achieved by adding various metallic oxides to the basic glass composition, but Tiffany's lengthy and often expensive researches led to more inventive and controllable use of chemically induced effects.*

*(3) Gallé also produced cameo glass, in which one colour was "cased" in another and then the outer surface cut to form the design. This cameo glass lampshade on a bronze base, made c. 1900, is a typically subtle flower form.*

3

4

*(5) Two bowls of painted and acid-etched glass by Daum of Nancy (1900-6) who followed and developed the tradition established by Emile Gallé and the Ecole de Nancy.*

5

# COLOURED GLASS

**(1)** *A selection of 19th-century English wine glasses showing a variety of colour techniques — staining, enamelling and overlaying — and* **(2)** *four different types of late 19th-century American coloured glass. These are, left to right: a peachblow bowl made at the Mount Washington Glass Works, New Bedford; a Wild Rose peachblow vase made at the New England Glass Co. of Cambridge, Massachussetts; a coral cruet by Hobbs, Brockunier & Co., Wheeling, West Virginia, and an Amberina vase from the New England Glass Co.*

1

2

3

**(3)** *A cranberry glass fruit or flower bowl, c. 1890. Cranberry glass maintained its popularity from about 1840 until the First World War and was used for decorative table ware of all sorts*

4

**(5)** *Three examples of Bohemian glass of the 1830s, left to right: a blue tumbler of the shape known as a* ranftbecher; *a stained ruby and yellow goblet with cut decoration on the stem and foot in the style of Friedrich Egermann of Blottendorf, and a yellow flashed beaker.*

5

**(4)** *A selection of coloured glass painted with figures of children in white enamel. This type of decoration, known as "Mary Gregory", is supposed to have originated with a certain Mary Gregory at the Boston & Sandwich Glass Co., but most examples were actually made in Bohemia.* **(6)** *An Amberina bottle made at the New England Glass Co., c. 1885, and a Rubina Verde bowl and opalescent hobnail vase, both made by Hobbs, Brockunier & Co., c. 1885.*

6

# GLASS TECHNIQUES

**(1)** *A late 19th-century cameo glass vase by Thomas Webb & Son of Stourbridge. The Woodall brothers, Thomas and George, specialized in this form of decoration; an outer layer of opaque white glass was fused to a coloured background and parts were removed with acid; the remaining white areas were carved in delicate relief. The cameo glass technique was used by John Northwood for his copy of the Portland Vase.*

**(2)** *A late 19th-century silvered glass goblet made by Varnish's patent method: a glass was blown in two layers, like a thermos flask, and the silvering and/or colour was introduced between the walls.*

*(3)* *A late-19th-century slag glass jug of the type made in vast quantities in the Tyneside area. Furnace waste from the steel works there was one of the ingredients, but not all such glass was of the opaque marbled or black variety — bright colours and clear glass were also pressed into decorative patterns and shapes. The largest producer was Sowerby but the output of two other Newcastle firms, Greener and Davidson, was considerable, and there were others. (4) An American opalescent pressed-glass sauce dish. Pressed glass, made for the masses, represents more accurately than most types both the range of ordinary domestic wares and the period's popular design themes. The techniques were first developed in America in the 1820s, exported to Europe in the 1830s, and eagerly embraced as a cheap substitute for cut glass.*

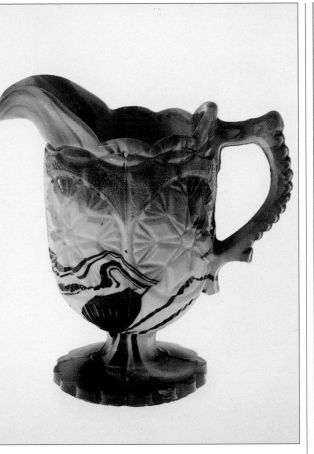

3

4

5

*(5)* *A mid-19th-century Bohemian stoppered bottled in opaline glass with gilt and enamelled decoration. Bohemia led the world in the production of coloured glass from about 1800-40, and besides the well-known stained and cased varieties, most of the popular European techniques were continued there in the second half of the century.*

# GLASS TECHNIQUES

*(1) A mid-19th-century jug and tumbler by Richardson of Stourbridge, part of a water set in clear glass enamelled with naturalistic irises in green and yellow. Richardson was one of the most progressive of Victorian glassmakers, supplying glass to Felix Summerly's Art Manufactures, some of which was designed by Felix Summerly (Henry Cole) himself.*

*(2) A vase of schmelzglas, made in imitation of hardstones by partially fusing glass of two or more colours randomly together. The technique was introduced in Bohemia in the early 19th century and this ormolu-mounted example, by Salviati of Venice, was exhibited at the 1862 International Exhibition in London.*

*(3) A late 19th-century "frigger" in the form of birds at a fountain. Such virtuoso exercises in spun glass were often made by craftsmen with glass left in the crucible at the end of the day, and were regarded as a workman's perks. "End of day" glass (known in America as "off-hand" glass) included novelties such as walking-sticks, pipes, small animals, rolling-pins and even fully rigged ships.*

2    3

*(4)* A 19th-century goblet elaborately gilded by J. Barbe of Stourbridge. Gilding was a popular form of decoration on Victorian glass. *(5)* Three millefiori *paperweights by (left to right) Baccarat, Clichy and St Louis, the three French factories whose products of the 1840-50 period have never been surpassed. Rods of coloured glass were fused together and then sliced, arranged to form a design and covered with domes of clear glass. The* millei-ori *technique was an ancient one, probably revived in Bohemia and Venice in the 1830s and then taken up with great success in France. French immigrants like Georges Bontemps, working in England after 1848, are likely to have introduced it to British craftsmen.*

4

6

5

*(6)* A three-branched candlestick of vaseline glass, a decorative type that developed from opaline in France and became popular in both England and America in the second half of the 19th century. The partial opacity was achieved by the addition of metallic oxides to the molten glass.

# GLASS FOR BUILDINGS

**(1)** *Stained-glass panels of Art Nouveau design behind the bar of the Philharmonic, Liverpool. The Victorian public house, with its elaborate carved wood fitments, stucco decoration, lavishly etched glass and* colourful tiles must have seemed a luxurious retreat indeed to the working class it was designed to serve.

2

1

3

**(2)** *The acid-etched bay window of Rea's Bar, Aberystwyth, typical of many late 19th-century public houses. Acid etching is seen at its most decorative in pub architecture.*

**(3)** *Stained-glass portraits adorn the windows of the Café Royal, Edinburgh.*

4

5

6

Arts and Crafts Movement led to its widespread use in domestic architecture *(5)*, as in this door panel of the 1880s. *(6) A convolvulus roundel of stained glass surrounded by rays of frosted glass: a typically decorative way of maintaining domestic privacy in the late 19th century.*

*(4) One of the stained-glass windows designed by Burne-Jones in 1870 for Christ Church, Oxford, and made by Powells of Whitefriars, leading manufacturers of decorative glass. The revival of interest in stained glass stimulated by the*

# GLOSSARY

**Acid-gilding** A method by which parts of a gilded surface could be given an incised matt finish by etching it with hydrofluoric acid. This technique of decorating porcelain with both matt and burnished gilding was developed at Minton in the 1860s.

**Aerography** The spraying of ground colour on ceramics by means of a type of airbrush, introduced in the 1890s.

**Antimacassar** A lace or embroidered drape for the back of a chair to protect the upholstery from macassar oil and other kinds of hair grease used by Victorian men.

**Aventurine glass** A gold-speckled effect made by mixing copper crystals with the glass in its molten state.

**Balloon-back** A type of chair, popular from the 1830s to the 1870s. The rounded back narrows towards the seat, giving an outline resembling a hot-air balloon.

**Barbotine** A way of decorating pottery with coloured slip, developed at the Sèvres factory by Ernest Chaplet in the 1870s and adopted widely for ornamenting tiles in the 1880s and 1890s.

**Barge ware** Brown-glazed teapots and other earthenwares with applied floral decoration and inscriptions, made in Derbyshire and sold on the canals. It is also known as Measham ware.

**Basse-taille** Translucent enamelling over engraved or engine-turned metal.

**Bentwood furniture** Mass-produced furniture, particularly chairs, of wood bent by steam into appropriate shapes. The process was introduced in the 1840s by Michael Thonet of Vienna.

**Biedermeier** The fashionable bourgeois style of Austria and Germany from about 1815 to 1848. The name comes from *bieder,* meaning plain and unpretentious, and Meier, a common German surname.

**Biscuit porcelain** Unglazed porcelain.

**Bois durci** An early plastic material made of fine sawdust bound with water and blood press-moulded into decorative shapes for medallions, brooches, small picture frames, boxes and applied ornament for furniture. It was invented and patented in London and Paris by Charles Lepage in 1855 and widely used for simulating ebony.

**Boulle work** The decoration of furniture in elaborate marquetry of brass and tortoiseshell, sometimes also with pewter, lapis lazuli and mother-of-pearl, introduced in the 16th century by André-Charles Boulle, *ébeniste* to Louis XIV. It was copied throughout the Victorian period, when it was sometimes known as "Buhl" work.

**Britannia metal** An alloy of tin, antimony and copper which was used as an alternative to pewter from about 1820 to 1850. It was sometimes electroplated (and marked EPBM) but was eventually superseded by nickel-silver.

**Bronzes d'ameublement** Small bronzes and ornamental metalwork for home decoration.

**Burmese glass** A late 19th-century decorative glass of greenish yellow shading to pink introduced at the Mount Washington Glass Co. in America and later made in England by Thomas Webb of Stourbridge.

**Bombe** The "blown-out" swollen shape of chests of drawers and other furniture of the Rococo period (and its revival).

**Bone china** A porcelain body modified by the addition of calcined bones and fired at a slightly lower temperature than true (hard-paste) porcelain. Its strength, whiteness and translucency have made it the preferred body of English porcelain manufacturers since the beginning of the 19th century.

**Cameo glass** Glass of one colour cased with another layer which is carved, engraved or etched to form the decoration.

**Canterbury** Originally a kind of supper trolley, but during the 19th century the name given to a low partitioned stand on castors for holding music books.

**Carton pierre** A type of papier mâché with whiting added, made in the 1880s in imitation of carved wood or moulded plaster.

**Cased (or overlay) glass** Glass of one colour covered with one or two others, with the decoration carved through them. The type was made in Bohemia from the early 19th-century and in England after 1845.

**Champlevé** Literally, "raised ground" — a form of enamelling in which the colours are laid in depressions and grooves scooped out of the metal surface of an object and then polished down to the same level.

**Chesterfield** A large low-backed, double-ended sofa with deep buttoned upholstery, introduced in the 1880s, and still popular today.

**Chromolithography** Printing in oil-based coloured inks from a separate stone for each colour was a development of the lithographic process, and became popular and cheap from the 1850s onwards. The results are also known as oleolithographs.

**Chryselephantine work** Figures of bronze or silver and ivory.

**Cire perdue** The ancient "lost wax" method of bronze casting used by many of the 19th century French *fondeurs.* A model was made in wax on a clay core and then covered with a clay mould. This was then baked, allowing the wax to run out and molten bronze to take its place.

**Cloisonné** Enamelling within *cloissons* or cells of wire soldered to the surface of an object.

**Close-plating** The covering of iron or steel flatware with a layer of silver foil. The technique was used from about 1809 to 1840, when it was superseded by electroplating.

**Clutha glass** The streaked and bubbled glass of organic form designed by Christopher Dresser and made by James Couper of Glasgow in the 1880s and '90s.

**Cranberry glass** Red-tinted glass made in large quantities from the 1840s onwards.

**Crystallo-ceramie** A process by which a porcelain cameo or painted plaque was enclosed within clear glass. It was practised in France, and then in England by Apsley Pellatt, who patented an improved process in 1819. It was also used in America, mainly for paperweights. Crystallo-ceramies are also known as cameo incrustations or (in America) as sulphides.

**Decalcomania** Decoration, mainly on glass or furniture, with applied prints or transferred pictures.

**Diaphanie** The imitation of stained glass by means of coloured paper applied to clear glass and varnished.

**Ebonizing** The blackening of wood to resemble ebony, fashionable for "art" furniture in the 1870s and 1880s.

**Electro-plating** The process of covering one metal with a thin layer of another by electrolysis. It was used a great deal for silver-plating on nickel (EPNS) from the 1840s onwards after George Elkington of Birmingham had discovered and developed the technique.

**Electro-typing** A related process to electro-plating, in which a layer of metal is deposited on the surface of a mould.

**Email ombrant (or lithophane)** A picture impressed into the clay body of, for example, a dish or the bottom of a mug, and then covered in transparent glaze. When held to the light the image appears in relief. Lithophanes were also known as Berlin transparencies.

**Epergne** A centrepiece for the dining table, usually branched, with vases for flowers or dishes for sweetmeats.

**Favrile** Tiffany's iridescent glass.

**Flashed glass** A similar technique to cased glass in which a thin film of one colour, usually red, was applied over another and then lightly engraved to form the decoration. The process was developed in Bohemia and later used in England.

**Flatbacks** 19th-century Staffordshire figures designed as chimney ornaments.

**Friggers** Glass novelties such as ships in bottles, walking sticks, bells, rolling pins and small animals. They were made by the glassworkers from "end of day glass" left in the crucible.

**German silver or nickel silver** An alloy of copper, zinc and nickel used as a basis for electro-plating; marked either EPGS (electroplated German silver) or EPNS (electro-plated nickel silver).

**Grand Rapids furniture** American mass-produced furniture, made in Grand Rapids, Michigan from the mid-19th century onwards.

**Grivoiseries** Pornographic scenes or writings on, for example, cigar cases, snuff boxes and other objects of *vertu*.

**Hyalith** An opaque red or black Bohemian glass made in the factory of Count von Buquoy.

**Jugenstil** "Youth style" — the German name for Art Nouveau.

**Lithophane** *see* **Email ombrant**.

**Lithyalin** An opaque coloured glass made to imitate semi-precious stones by Friedrich Egermann of Bohemia.

**Lustres** Glass vases hung with cut glass prisms — hence their alternative name, "prism vases" — popular in the middle decades of the 19th century.

**Mauchline ware** Souvenir woodwares bearing transfer-printed topographical views or tartan decoration, made in Scotland.

**Opaline glass** Translucent glass made partially opaque by adding tin oxide or bone ash, with or without colouring oxides, to the molten metal.

**Parian porcelain** A type of biscuit porcelain resembling the white marble of Paros, developed in England in the 1840s. Later, tinted varieties were also produced.

**Pâte-de-verre** Moulded glass made from powdered glass mixed with glue. The technique was developed in France at the end of the 19th century.

**Pâte-sur-pâte** Decoration in low relief, painted and carved in layers of clay slip applied to a porcelain (often parian) surface.

**Pietra dura** Marquetry of coloured hardstones.

**Pliqué-à-jour** Enamelling technique in which the colours are confined by wires as in *cloisonné*, but not backed, so they remain translucent.

**Pressed glass** Glass decorated by being pressed into a mould at its molten stage. The technique was developed in America in the 1820s for making cheap substitutes for cut glass, but was later widely adopted in Europe.

**Prie-dieu** A devotional chair consisting of a low seat and a padded top rail.

**Registration marks** Diamond-shaped marks used on metal, wood, glass and earthenware between 1842 and 1883 to record the details registered in the Patent Office Registry of Designs. Letters and numbers in the different compartments of the diamond give information about the year, month and day of manufacture, the type of item and the batch number (which identifies the manufacturer). From 1884 to 1909 a simple system of registered numbers replaced the diamond mark. All can be traced in the Public Record Office in London.

**Roycroft Shops** American outlets for craftsman-made furniture, textiles, pottery and metalwork made by "Roycrofters" — the disciples of Elbert Hubbard and the Arts and Crafts Movement in the 1890s.

**Sang-de-boeuf** Crimson (ox-blood) glaze used by the Chinese and rediscovered by the English potter Bernard Moore towards the end of the 19th century.

**Satin glass** English and American "art" glass of the second half of the 19th century with a matt surface effect induced by exposing it to the vapour of hydrofluoric acid.

**Satsuma ware** 19th-century Japanese earthenware busily decorated with "brocaded" and floral designs, which were imported in large quantities and copied in Europe.

**Sgraffito** "Scratched" decoration on a pottery surface, usually through a layer of slip to show the ground colour underneath.

**Slag glass** A type of press-moulded coloured glass, first made in Northeast England, incorporating slag or furnace waste from the steel works there.

**Stevengraphs** Woven silk pictures made by Thomas Stevens of Coventry from 1854 onwards.

**Stile Liberty** The Italian term for Art Nouveau.

**Tantalus** A locking wooden holder for decanters.

**Tinsel pictures** Portrait engravings, generally of actors and actresses, embellished with metallic foil, popular in the 1830s and '40s.

**Tole ware or tole peinte** The French equivalent of japanned iron or tin.

**Transfer-printing** The technique of decorating ceramics with impressions taken from engraved plates.

**Troubadour style** The French revived Gothic style of the 1830s and '40s.

**Vaseline glass** A yellow opaline glass originating in France and made in England and America in the second half of the 19th century.

**Vienna Secession** The Austrian anti-establishment art group of the turn of the century which had a formative influence first on Art Nouveau and later on the development of the Modern Movement.

**Xylonite** One of the earliest plastics, an artificial celluloid, invented by Parkes of Birmingham in 1856 and used for boxes, picture frames, piano keys and small objects.

**Zinc or spelter** A metal used in alloys such as brass and also as a substitute for bronze in decorative metalwork.

# INDEX

Page numbers in *italic* refer to the illustrations and captions

# CREDITS

Abbreviations used: t = top; l = left; b = bottom; c = centre; r = right

Architectural Association Slide library: 6, 16, 17, 18 22 tl, 25 tr, 26 t, 29 tl, r, br, 32 tl, br, 34, 35 tr, 36 t & bl (c/o AA/F.R. Yerbury) 40, 45 b, 68 tl, 69 bl, 147 tr, 175 tl, 184 tl
Author's collection: 9t, 174-5 b
Chloë Alexander: 19
American School of Classical Studies, Athens: 142 l
Art Institute of Chicago: 56
Paul Atterbury: 156 t, 165 tr
Barnardo's Photograph library: 95 t
Bonhams: 65 bl
N. Bloom & Son Ltd: 141 t, 130 tl
The Bridgeman Art Library: 11, 25 tl, 54, 59, 60 r, 61 tl, 62 tl, 63 l, c, br, 65 tl, 66 t, 67, 68 bl, 69 t, b, l, bl, 70 t, 71 t, 76 tr, 77 tl, 78 r, 81 t, 82 l, 83 l, c, r, 86, 87, 89 r, 90 t, 91 br, 103 b, 104-5, 106 br, 107 r, 110 b, 121 r, 130 bl, 132 tl, r, 142 t, br, 143 tl, 148 t, bl, 149 tl, r, b, 150, 151 tl, 154, 160 t, b, 161 b, 162 tl, 163, 164, 165 tl, 166 r, 167 tl, 169 r, b, 170 t, bl, 171 br, 173 tr, l, 176 tl, br, 177 c, b, 178, 179 b, 180 l, r, 181 tl, r, 182 tl, r, 183
The British Architectural Library: 8, 22 br, 142 bl
Christie's Colour Library: 62 t, 87 br, 911, 102 tl, 151b

Chicago Historical Society: 96 tr
Cincinnati Art Museum: 94 tr
Freda Clinch: Title page, 42, 91 l
Corning Museum of Glass: 159
The Colman Collection: 153 t
The Design Council: 58 l, 76 b
Alastair Duncan: 158
E.T. Archive: 42
English Heritage: 121 l
The Mary Evans Picture Library: 5, 411, 53tl, 106 tr, 107 1, 108 tl, 111 tl, 112, 113, 114, 116, 117, 122 bl, 123 t, bl, 124 tl, 125 b, r, 126 tr, 127 tr, 128 r, 129 bl, 130 br, 131 bl, 167 b
The Fine Art Society London Ltd: 100, 100-101 b, 101 r, 103 b, 151 tr
The Colouste Gulbenkian Foundation: 126 bl
Garrard & Co. Ltd, Crown Jewellers: 144 tl
Haslam and Whiteway: 146 br
John Hannavy Picture Collection: 91 tr, 98, 99, 102 tr, b, 124 br
Sonia Halliday Photographs: 185 tr
Angelo Hornack Photograph Library: 24 t, 28 r, 61 b, 64 l, 66 bl, 70-71, 74 r, 75 tr, 147 b, 160 tr, 161 tl, 162 r, 165 bl, r, 168 r, 170 tr, 171 tr, 176 tr, 179 tl, r, 181 b, 182 br
B.E.C. Howarth-Loomes Collection: 98 l
The Illinois State History Society 68 tr
Lankesters: 128 l

A.F. Kersting: 14
Lenswork: 22 tr, 23 t, 26 br, 27 t, 28 l, 30 bl, 31, 32 tr, 37 l, tr
Liberty & Co. Ltd: 81 br, 136
Lunn Antiques: 83
The Mansell Collection Ltd: 20 tl, br, 21 b, 24 b, 25 br, 45 tl, 46 tl, r, 47 t, bl, 50 tl, 110 t, 120 bl
Middlesex Polytechnic Silver Studios Collection 78 b, 79 t, 80
The William Morris Gallery: 89 tl
The National Army Museum: 165 tr
The National Gallery of Scotland: 100 tr
Peter Newark's Western Americana and Historical Pictures: 6, 47 , 84, 88, 90, 93 t, bl, r, 96 br, 97 tl, b
Norfolk Museum Service: 146 tr
Robert Opie: 108 r
Private Collection: 103 tr
Phillips Fine Art Auctioneers: 41 r, 53 tr, 122 tl, r, 123 cr, 124 c, 124 c, 125 bl, 130 tr, 134 tl, r, b, 133 bl
The Royal Library Windsor Castle: 120 r
The Royal Photographic Society: 84, 88, 90, 93 t, bl, r, 96 br, 97 tl,b, 101 t
Royal Doulton Historical Promotions: 167 r, 172, 173 bl, 174 tr
Derek Roberts Antiques: 71 b
Arthur Sanderson & Sons Ltd: 78 tl, 79b

Sotheby's London: 62 br, 64 tr, 74 l, 77 br, 82 r, 120 tl, 123 br, 124 bl, 132 bl,r, 133 t, br, 134 tc, 135 tr, 141 b, 145 bl, 153 tl, bl, r, 172, 177 tl
Sotheby's Sussex: 71 cr 146, 138, 140, 147 tl, 148 tr, 152
Spinks & Sons: 144
Topham Picture Library: 23, 26 br, 27 br, 33 l, 36 tr, 44 tl bl, r, 66 bl, 69 tl, 174 tl, 184 tr, br
Victoria & Albert Museum, London: 13, 20 bl, 35 br, 57 t, 58 r, 64 b, 70 b, 76 tl, 143 tr, 144 tr, 145 tl, r, 166 l
Wedgwood: 156, 157
Elizabeth Whiting Association: 66 br
Wolverhampton Art Galleries & Museums: Bantock House Museum: 146 bl

Although we have made every effort to trace and acknowledge all copyright holders, Quarto would like to apologize if there should be any omissions.